Cooking is a journey of creation. From idea to reality. To look good and taste amazing. A passion, an obsession—but where do you draw the line and move on?

A cheese souffle. The recipe is direct from a two-Michelin-starred chef. My first attempts were a bit messy, eventually not bad but not perfect. When I thought I'd cracked it, it was pointed out by the chef that it had collapsed slightly and actually wasn't right. It needed work and practicing over and over. I practiced some more to understand the process, and once it looked good, I was quite happy with my efforts. The final comment, almost dismissively, was "It does look better, but what does it taste like?".

Here's what I've learned:

Ingredients: buy seasonally, locally, organic and the best you can.

Presentation: practice practice practice.

Taste: the key, really, once you have the first two elements sorted.

Summary: This is my attempt at fine dining from a home kitchen, aiming for the stars and ending up somewhere else. But I love cooking, and I love pushing myself. I'm still learning, but I'm still having fun. Each dish is a work in progress.

This is good food cooked badly... Bon Appetit!

Contents

Starters & Small Stuff

Croustade of Venison	4
Scallop & Celeriac Sauce	6
Scallop Albufera	10
Cashew Salad	14
Coleslaw	16
Truffle Egg	18
Salad of Micro Herbs & Lime	20
Crusty Bread	24
Salmon Skin, Cucumber & Almond	28
Prawn & Salmon Skin Open Sandwich	32
Mussels, Pine Needles & Coffee	36
Frites Thermidor	38
Crispy Pasta "Carbonara"	42
Cheese Souffle	44
Lamb Rillette & Cherry	48
Prawn Cocktail	52

Contents

Parmesan & Macadamia	56
Prawn & Toasted Rice Consomme	60
Grilled Octopus & Fava Puree	64
Black Malloreddus Carbonara	68
Ham & Cambridge Sauce	72
Mackerel on Toast	74
Scotch Egg & Chilli Crack	78
Roast Chicken & Truffle Sandwich	82
Tuna Tartare & Fennel Seed Cracker	86
Basque Style Chorizo Croquettes	90
Aubergine, Ginger & Rye Bread	92
Wild Garlic Pesto Flatbread	96
Crab Crumpet	98
Potato Pave	102
Brandade & Sourdough	106
Foie Royale & Brioche	110
Chicken Katsu Bao	114

Contents

Mains & Big Stuff

Wood Pigeon & Autumn Vegetables	124
Venison & Cauliflower Cheese	128
Singapore Style Chilli Crab	134
Lamb, Aubergine & Feta	138
Lemon Chicken	142
Cod & Coriander Veloute	146
Short Rib Pappadelle & Tomato Sauce	150
Ballotine of Pheasant	154
Pork, Prunes & Onion Soubise	158
Lamb Burger	162
Steak, Miso & Mushroom	166
Risotto of Squash & Gorgonzola	170
Sea Bass & Peanut Sauce	174
Monkfish Vadouvan	178
Beef, Tamari & Shiitake	182
Beef & Basil Meatballs	186
Sage & Bacon Ravioli	190
Tuna, Gooseberry & Mayo	194

Contents

Lamb, Spiced Red Pepper & Potatoes	198
Wagyu, Sesame Hollandaise & Nori	202
Gnocchi Parisienne	208
Duck & Squash	212
Pork Belly & Onion Veloute	216
Salmon & Rose Beurre 'Blanc'	220
Monkfish, Pork & Black Garlic	224
Monkfish Curry & Cauliflower	228
Wagyu Lasagna & Sauce Buccaneer	232
Inman Ramen	236

Contents

Desserts & Sweet Stuff

Pecan Ice Cream & Dark Chocolate	244
Jerusalem Artichoke Fudge	248
Soho Bun	250
Scottish Tablet Sundae	252
Pear & Ginger Crumble with Dark Chocolate	256
Lemon Tart	260
Amaretto & Ginger Cheesecake	264
Chocolate & Orange Fondant	266
Madeleines of Lemon & Thyme	268
Lime & Mint Panna Cotta	270
Lemon & Pistachio Financier	272
London Cheesecake	274
Shortbread, Jam & Burnt Meringue	276
Amaretti & Basque Cheesecake	280
Tarte Bordaloue	284

Contents

Date Cake & Miso Caramel	288
Fig & Orange Cheesecake	292
Chocolate & Fig Oat Cookies	296
Pistachio Cake & Creme Chiboust	298
Pain Perdu & Chocolate	302
Cinnamon Cracker & Cheddar	306
Meringue, Coffee & Autumn Fruits	310
Crema Catalana	314
Pistachio Tiramisu	316
Champagne Truffles	320
Pineapple & Lime	322
Pink Pralines	324
Choux au Craquelin	328
Chocolate Marquise & Miso Cremeux	332
Lemon Parfait & Meringue	336

Starters & Small Stuff

Croustade of Venison

Scallop & Celeriac Sauce

Scallop Albufera

Cashew Salad

Coleslaw

Truffle Egg

Salad of Micro Herbs & Lime

Crusty Bread

Salmon Skin, Cucumber & Almond

Prawn & Salmon Skin Open Sandwich

Mussels, Pine Needles & Coffee

Frites Thermidor

Crispy Pasta "Carbonara"

Cheese Souffle

Lamb Rillette & Cherry

Prawn Cocktail

Parmesan & Macadamia

Prawn & Toasted Rice Consomme

Grilled Octopus & Fava Puree

Black Malloreddus Carbonara

Ham & Cambridge Sauce

Mackerel on Toast

Scotch Egg & Chilli Crack

Roast Chicken & Truffle Sandwich

Tuna Tartare & Fennel Seed Cracker

Basque Style Chorizo Croquettes

Aubergine, Ginger & Rye Bread

Wild Garlic Pesto Flatbread

Crab Crumpet

Potato Pave

Brandade & Sourdough

Foie Royale & Brioche

Katsu Chicken Bao

Croustade of Venison

42g plain flour
55ml beer
17g dashi
5g sugar
5g clarified butter
5g corn starch (Crytex)
21g eggs
Oil for deep frying

50g venison
½ tsp salt
5g shallot
5g beetroot, pickled from a jar, plus some of the liquid
5g celeriac
Beetroot ketchup , see wood pigeon recipe
1 tsp Worcestershire sauce
Micro greens

Tart shell

One day in advance, combine the flour, beer, dashi, sugar, butter, corn starch, and eggs in a blitzer and leave to rest in the fridge overnight. The next day, re-blitz the mixture if necessary to loosen.
Heat the oil to 180 degrees in a small sauce pan.
Dip an iron into the oil then dip into the batter, then back into the oil, and crisp the batter. Carefully remove them and reserve in a low oven to retain the crispiness.

Venison

Finely and evenly slice the venison into 1 cm cubes, add the salt, and mix well.
Finely slice the shallot, beetroot, and celeriac as small as possible and add to a small bowl with some beetroot pickle liquid. Leave for around 10 minutes, and then drain the vegetables.
Add the vegetables and Worcestershire sauce to the venison and gently stir to combine thoroughly.
Spoon the venison mixture into a tart shell and top with some beetroot ketchup and microgreens.

Scallop & Celeriac Sauce

King scallop, plus shell for serving
1 tbsp butter
Salt

Scallops

Remove the scallop from the shell. Heat a little oil in a pan and then sear the scallops on one side and then add the butter; insert a small skewer into the scallop to check it's cooked through—the skewer should be warm. Let the scallop rest and baste with the butter. Before serving, slice the scallops into about five pieces and season lightly.

Celeriac
150 ml vegetable stock
Salt
Lemon juice
1 tbsp butter
2 tbsp double cream

Celeriac sauce

Peel and dice half of the celeriac. Add the diced celeriac to a pan with the vegetable stock and cook until the celeriac is soft. Drain the celeriac and reserve some of the cooking liquid. Add the celery, salt, and lemon juice to a blender and blitz until smooth; add some reserved stock if need be to achieve a runny sauce consistency. Return the sauce to a pan and add the cream. Heat gently and check the taste; adjust with salt and/or lemon juice.

8-10 Chestnut mushrooms

Mushroom powder

Pre heat the oven to 120 degrees.

Finely slice the mushrooms and heat in an oven for around 45 minutes until dried out and crispy. Remove from the oven and allow to cool.

Add the mushrooms to a spice grinder and blitz to a fine powder.

Crispy leeks

1 baby leek

Heat some oil to 170 degrees in a small saucepan. Finely slice the leeks into matchsticks, about 5cm in length and dry out on a piece of kitchen roll.

Drop the leeks into the oil and fry for around 10 seconds until crispy.

To serve:

Add the sliced scallop back to the scallop shell.
Spoon around some of the celeriac sauce.
Sprinkle some mushroom powder over the scallops.
Top the scallops with some crispy leeks.

Scallop Albufera

King scallops, 2 or 3
Oil
1 tbsp butter
Salt

Scallop

Pan fry the scallop until seared on one side and warm throughout; check with a metal skewer. Add the butter to the pan and baste and then leave to rest. Slice in half before serving and season.

15g butter (+10g to finish)
15g flour
200ml chicken stock
10g crème fraiche
1 tsp Madeira
1 tbsp glace de viande (reduced veal stock)
2 tbsp red pepper
30g red pepper, diced
1 tsp shallots, diced
½ tsp lemon zest
Salt
White pepper

Sauce Albufera

Start by making a sauce supreme. Melt the butter in a sauce pan and add the flour and stir to combine to make a roux.
Gradually add the chicken stock and keep stirring until the sauce has thickened.
Add the crème fraiche and the madeira and stir to finish the sauce supreme.
Next, make the red pepper butter by combining the butter, the red pepper, the shallots, and lemon zest.
To finish the Albufera sauce, bring the sauce supreme back to a simmer, then whisk in the glace de viande.
Next, add the red pepper butter and then reduce to reach the desired consistency.
Check the taste and add salt and/or pepper as required.

Parsley
Micro greens

To serve:

Spoon some sauce into the middle of a small plate or bowl.
Add the sliced scallop and top with a little chopped parsley and micro greens.

Cashew Salad

Cashew cream:

Blitz together all the ingredients until smooth and creamy. Pass through a sieve.

55g roast cashew nuts (save a couple for finely chopping to finish)
50ml water
2 tbsp olive oil
2 tbsp lemon juice
1 garlic clove, blanched
½ tsp salt
½ tsp sugar

Crispy Potatoes

Toss the potatoes in the garlic powder and soy sauce.

3 new potatoes, par boiled and roasted until crispy
½ tsp garlic powder
1 tsp soy sauce

To serve:

Add the cashew cream to a plate. Place the potatoes onto the cream and then carefully add the avocado and crispy bacon.
Add the crispy onions and lime zest and finish with some coriander leaves, micro herbs and chopped cashew nuts.

¼ avocado, diced
Crispy bacon
Lime zest
Crispy onions
Coriander leaves, finely chopped
Micro herbs

Coleslaw

Baby gem lettuce, outer leaves
50g red cabbage, thinly sliced
50g cabbage, thinly sliced
50g carrot, peeled and thinly sliced
45g mayo
15g sour cream
1 tsp sugar
1 tsp lemon juice
Micro herbs
Salt

Place the cabbage and carrot into a colander (do not mix at this stage) and sprinkle over a little salt.

Leave for 20 minutes, then squeeze out any excess liquid.

Mix together the mayo, sour cream, sugar and lemon juice, then fold the drained cabbage and carrot through the mayo mixture.

Spoon this mixture into a lettuce leaf and top with some micro herbs.

Truffle Egg

1 egg
1/2 tsp mustard
1 tsp grated truffle
Pinch salt
Extra black truffle, for grating to finish

Boil the egg for 7 minutes and then remove from the pan, place in cold water.
Once cooled, peel the shell from the egg and then slice off the top of the egg.
Remove the yolk from the egg and place in a bowl.
Add the mustard, black truffle, and salt to the egg yolk and mix and mash together with a fork.
Place the egg yolk mixture into a piping bag with a star nozzle inserter.
Pipe the egg yolk mixture back into the egg and serve in an egg cup.

Salad of Micro Herbs & Lime

Micro herbs

Selection of micro herbs (kale, clover, broccoli, pea shoots)
Spinach leaves, finely chopped

Gently mix the leaves together until fully combined.

Lime vinaigrette

Zest and juice from 1 lime
1/2 tsp Dijon mustard
Pinch of salt
Pinch of garlic powder
1/2 tsp maple syrup
1 tbsp olive oil

Mix together all of the ingredients until fully combined.
Check the taste and adjust with salt and/or lime juice as required.

Pickled radish

2 radishes
25ml white wine vinegar
25ml water
5g salt
5g sugar
Few sprigs of thyme

Slice the radish as finely as possible.
In a small bowl, combine the white wine vinegar, water, salt, sugar, and thyme.
Add the radish to the pickling liquid and leave for 20 minutes.
Remove the radish and leave to drain any excess liquid on kitchen paper.

Parmesan
Pork scratchings
Micro herbs

To serve

Take fine slices of the Parmesan and cut into circles with a small pastry cutter roughly the same size as the slices of radish..
Add the salad leaves to a bowl and spoon over some vinaigrette.
Top with the radish, Parmesan and scratchings.
To finish, add a few micro herbs.

Crusty Bread

This bread recipe is cooked in a spring oven.

Dough

7g active dry yeast
15g honey
225g lukewarm water
6g salt
205g plain flour
102g white spelt flour

Mix together the yeast, honey and water in a large mixing bowl. Leave for 5 minutes until the mixture is foamy.
Add the flours to the yeast mixture and mix with a wooden spoon until the dough starts to come together.
Add the salt and continue mixing until no dry flour remains and the dough is loose and a little sticky.
Cover the bowl with a tea towel and leave for just over an hour and the dough should rise and double in size.
When the dough has risen, lightly flour a work surface and tip out the dough. Do not knock the dough back.
Shape the dough into a round loaf by folding over the edges like an envelope. Repeat this several times until the dough stiffens slightly; turn the dough over and place back into a bowl lined with flour (the dough should be seam side down) and cover and let rise for 30 minutes.

Baking

While the dough is, heat the oven to 220 degrees and place the spring oven (filled with 150 ml of water and the lid on) into the oven.

When the dough is ready, carefully pull out the spring oven and tip in the dough (seam side up). Bake for 30 minutes with the lid on. Then remove the lid, reduce the oven to 200 degrees, and cook for another 12 minutes until golden.

Remove from the oven, transfer the loaf to a wire rack, and cool before slicing.

Salmon Skin, Cucumber & Almond

Salmon skin

Salmon skin
Oil, for frying
Salt

Neatly cut the salmon skin into rectangles about 8x4cm.
Heat the oil in a small saucepan and then drop in the salmon skin until crispy.
Remove and drain and then lightly season before assembling.

Cucumber

¼ cucumber
2 tbsp water
1 tbsp white wine vinegar
1 tsp sugar
1 tsp salt
1 tsp dill

Finely slice the cucumber and cut each slice in half, then half again to leave quarter circles.
Take half of the cucumber pieces and put to one side.
The other half, place in a bowl with the water, white wine vinegar, sugar, salt and dill. Mix well and leave for 15 minutes.
After 15 minutes, remove the cucumber and drain on kitchen paper.

Almond cream

75g chopped almonds, lightly toasted
½ clove garlic, blanched and crushed
25g olive oil
1 tsp lemon juice
1 tsp red wine vinegar
Pinch of salt
Water, as needed

Place all of the ingredients into a blitzer and blitz until very smooth.
If the mixture is too thick, add a couple of drops of water at a time until you achieve a nice, creamy texture.
Place the almond cream into a piping bag.

Dill
Almond, very finely chopped

To serve

On a piece of salmon skin, neatly arrange the cucumber, alternating between pickled and non-pickled pieces.
Dot some almond cream onto the cucumber.
Sprinkle over a little of the finely chopped almonds.
Finish by placing some dill onto the almond cream.

Prawn & Salmon Skin Open Sandwich

Bread

Slice of crusty bread, see 'Crusty Bread' recipe
Olive oil

Brush the bread lightly with oil and then toast in a frying pan until pale golden.

Prawns

Prawns, heads and shells removed
Beef fat
Salt

In a frying pan, heat the beef fat and then fry the prawns until cooked.
Remove the prawns and beef fat and rest in a shallow baking tray.
With a blow torch, lightly colour the prawns. While resting, spoon over the beef fat occasionally and slice each prawn into 3 or 4 pieces then season before serving.

Lemongrass and mint mayonnaise

2 egg yolks
1 tsp Dijon mustard
Pinch of salt
Pinch of white pepper
250ml sunflower oil
2 tsp lemon juice
1 tbsp finely chopped mint leaves
1 stalk lemongrass, finely chopped

Start by infusing the oil with the lemongrass.
Crush and finely chop the lemongrass and add it to a pan with the sunflower oil. Gently heat the oil and leave to infuse for about an hour.
Blitz and strain the oil, then pass through a fine sieve and reserve and cool completely. Whisk together the egg yolks and mustard in a bowl, then add the salt and pepper.

Add the lemongrass oil a drop at a time and whisk until fully combined.
Once the yolks and oil are coming together, add the oil a bit more at a time and keep whisking.
When fully combined, whisk in the lemon juice and mint leaves.
Place into a piping bag.

Salmon skin crumb

Salmon skin
Oil, for frying
Salt

Heat the oil in a pan and then gently fry the skin until crispy.
Remove and drain.
Once cooled, break up the skin into small irregular pieces and season lightly.

To serve

Mint leaves, finely chopped

Take one piece of bread and add some chopped prawns.
Drizzle over the mayonnaise and then generously sprinkle over the salmon skin.
Finish with some mint leaves.

Mussels, Pine Needles & Coffee

Mussels

250g mussels
1 celery stalk, stem bark removed, diced (retain any leaves)
2 or 3 small pine leaf twigs, lightly rinsed
100ml white wine
5g dashi powder

In a sauce pan, add all the ingredients and bring to a boil, then reduce to a simmer. Cover the pan and cook until all the mussels have opened.
Remove and discard the pine twigs.
Remove the mussels from the shells and return to the cooking liquid.

Parmesan tuile

2 tbsp grated Parmesan

Pre heat the oven to 180 degrees.
Add the parmesan onto to an ovenproof silicone mat and cook for 5 minutes. Remove from the oven and carefully remove the tuile from the mat.

To serve:

1 tsp espresso powder
Celery leaves, see above

Add the mussels, celery and sauce to a shallow bowl.
Dust the mussels with espresso powder and then finish with the Parmesan tuile and celery leaves.

Frites Thermidor

Chips

2 Maris piper potato
Salt
1 small piece kombu
Oil for roasting and frying

Peel the potatoes then use a corer to create tubes of even length.
Gently boil the potatoes for about 5 minutes until softened in a pan of salted water with the kombu.
Drain and allow to steam dry.
Pre heat the oven to 160 degrees.
In a baking tray, add a little oil and then add the potatoes and bake for 25 minutes, turning a couple of times.
Remove the potatoes from the oven and allow to cool.
Heat some oil in a small sauce pan to 180 degrees and then carefully deep fry the potatoes until golden. Remove, drain and lightly season.

Thermidor sauce

1 tbsp butter
½ shallot, finely chopped
100ml lobster or fish stock
20ml Noilly Prat
15ml double cream
¼ tsp English mustard
1 tsp chopped fine herbs (chervil, parsley, tarragon)
1 tsp lemon juice
10g finely grated parmesan

In a pan, add the butter and shallots and cook until soft but not coloured.
Add the stock and Noily Prat then reduce by at least half until well thickened.
Add the cream and mustard and stir through.
Add the herbs and lemon juice.
Transfer the sauce to a small oven proof dish and then add the grated parmesan.
Place under a grill (or blowtorch) to melt the cheese.

Finely chopped parsley
Parmesan for grating

To serve:

Add the chips to a plate and then either place the sauce alongside or spoon it over the chips.
Finish with some parsley and grated parmesan.

Crispy Pasta "Carbonara"

50g semol flour
25ml warm water
Pinch salt
1 tsp olive oil
Truflle salt

Crispy pasta

Mix the flour, water and salt and knead for 5 minutes. Rest for 30 minutes. When ready roll out the dough to the second thinnest setting on the pasta machine. Cut to the desired shape.
Heat some water in a saucepan and season. Cook the pasta for 2 minutes and then remove and drain. Reserve some pasta water.
Line the pasta on a grill pan and brush over the olive oil. Place under the grill for a couple of minutes, and when the pasta starts to colour and rise, turn over and grill the other side. Remove, drain, and finish with some truffle salt.

Carbonara style sauce

20g bacon lardons, finely chopped
1 egg yolk
10g grated Parmesan
1 tsp lemon juice
1/4 garlic clove, grated
Black pepper

Fry the bacon in a pan.
In a bowl, mix the egg yolk, parmesan, lemon juice, and garlic to form a paste. Add the egg paste to the pan with the bacon and cook gently and slowly. Finish with a little black pepper.

To serve

Add the carbonara sauce to a ramekin and serve alongside the crispy pasta.

Cheese Soufflé

40g grated cheddar cheese
1 egg, separated
13g butter
13g flour
75ml milk, warmed
Extra butter, to line the ramekins
Grana Padano, grated, to line the ramekins
Salt
White pepper
25ml double cream
Chives
1 tbsp white wine vinegar
2 tbsp olive oil
Black truffle, optional

Makes 2-3 soufflés':

Preheat the oven to 125 degrees.
Grease a soufflé mould with a little butter and dust with the grated Grana Padano.
Make a roux by melting the butter in a pan and then whisking in the flour.
Gradually add the warmed milk while whisking and then allow to cook for 3 minutes.
Whisk in half of the cheese and then season well with salt and pepper.
Allow to cool slightly, and then whisk in the egg yolk.
In a separate bowl, whisk the egg white very slowly until stiff, and then fold into the cheese mixture.
Spoon into the ramekin until about half full, or just under.
Place the soufflé mould into a baking dish filled with enough water to go about 1/3 of the way up the soufflé mould and cook for 27 minutes.
Once cooked, turn out the soufflés and place into an ovenproof dish.
Turn the oven up to 150 degrees.
Pour over the cream and sprinkle with the remaining cheese, and then bake for another 8 minutes.

Make a dressing by mixing together the vinegar, oil and some finely chopped chives. Season lightly.

To serve:

Whilst hot, drizzle over a some dressing and some extra chives.
Finish with some grated black truffle if using and serve immediately

Lamb Rillette & Cherry

500g lamb shoulder
2 tbsp olive oil
Salt
Pepper
50ml red wine
½ onion, chopped
½ carrot, chopped
½ stalk celery, chopped
1 garlic clove
1 bay leaf
5 black peppercorns
Few thyme sprigs
Few rosemary sprigs
Small bunch of parsley
4 tbsp butter

Lamb

Preheat the oven to 160 degrees.
Heat the olive oil in a frying pan.
Season the lamb with salt and pepper.
Add the lamb to the pan and brown on all sides.
Place the lamb into a deep ovenproof dish.
Deglaze the frying pan with the wine and then pour over the lamb.
Add the onion, carrot, celery and garlic to the pan and fry until golden brown.
Add the vegetables to the lamb, followed by the herbs and butter. If necessary, add a little more oil to cover the lamb.
Place a lid on the dish and cook for about 2 hours or until the lamb is tender enough to pull apart with a fork.
Allow the lamb to cool for about 30 minutes.
Remove the lamb and strain from the fat.
Pull the lamb apart and add back 1 tbsp of the strained fat and stir to evenly distribute.
Store the lamb in a jar until needed.

Crackers

50g flour
Pinch white pepper
Pinch salt
Pinch sugar
7½ ml olive oil
30ml water, cold

Preheat the oven to 200 degrees.
Mix all of the ingredients except the water until well combined.
Add the water and mix to form a dough.
Roll out the dough as thinly as possible and then cut to the desired shape.
Place on baking paper and cook for 4 minutes; turn over and cook for another 4 minutes.
Once ready, turn off the oven, but leave the crackers to completely dry out (about one hour).

Cherry barbecue sauce

¼ onion, chopped
1 tsp butter
½ garlic clove, crushed
100g cherries, pitted and roughly chopped
25g ketchup
40g brown sugar
25ml rice vinegar
½ tsp Worcestershire sauce
Pinch white pepper
1 tsp mirin

Add the onion and butter to saucepan and cook gently until the onions are softened.
Add the garlic and cook for 1 minute.
Add all the remaining ingredients except the mirin and cook over a low heat for 15 minutes.
Allow to cool, add the mirin and then blitz until smooth and pass through a sieve.
Transfer to a squeezy bottle or piping bag.

To serve:

Spread a good amount of the lamb over a cracker and then squeeze over some sauce.

Prawn Cocktail

Per serving:

Prawns

6-8 king prawns
Optional: 1 extra prawn, unpeeled and head left on
1 tbsp beef fat
Salt

Peel the 6-8 king prawns and de-vein.
Heat the beef fat in a small pan and then cook the prawns, including the unpeeled prawn, turning once until you achieve a slight char on one side.
Remove from the pan, drain and lightly season.

Marie Rose sauce

2 tbsp mayonnaise
1 tbsp ketchup
¼ tsp Worcestershire sauce
1 tsp lemon juice
½ tsp brandy
Pinch salt
Pinch white pepper
Pinch paprika

Add all of the ingredients except the paprika to a small bowl and mix well until fully combined.
Check the taste and adjust as necessary.
Sprinkle over the paprika to finish.

Avocado salad

2 cherry, or small, tomatoes, halved
2 1cm slices of cucumber, diced
Sherry vinegar
1 tbsp sugar
1 tsp salt
½ avocado, mashed with a fork
1 tbsp lime juice
1 tsp lemon juice

In a small bowl, add the sherry vinegar, sugar and salt and mix well.
Add the tomatoes and cucumber to the bowl and leave for 20 minutes.
Remove the tomatoes and cucumber and drain on a piece of kitchen paper.
In another bowl, add the avocado, lime juice and lemon juice and mix well.
Fold in the pickled cucumber and tomatoes.

To serve:

Baby gem lettuce, 3 outer leaves

In a small bowl or glass, add the lettuce leaves.
Spoon in some of the avocado salad and top with half of the prawns.
Spoon in some of the Marie Rose sauce and top everything with the remaining prawns.
Finish with the final unpeeled prawn, if using.

Parmesan & Macadamia

Per serving:

Parmesan tuile

15g grated parmesan
Bronze powder, optional

Preheat the oven to 180 degrees.
Carefully place the grated parmesan over an upturned small bowl, ramekin, or tart case.
Place in the oven and cook for 7 minutes; the parmesan should melt and mold around the upturned bowl.
Remove from the oven and allow to cool.
With care, gently remove the tuile and dust with bronze powder if using.

Parmesan and black truffle sauce

10g butter
10g flour
100ml milk
15g grated parmesan
5g grated black truffle
Pinch salt
Pinch pepper

In a saucepan, melt the butter then add the flour, whisking continuously.
Slowly and gradually add the milk and whisk until thickened.
Add the parmesan, black truffle, salt and pepper and stir until fully melted and combined.

30g macadamia nuts
1 tbsp Worcestershire sauce
½ tsp grated black truffle

Macadamia nuts

Finely chop the nuts.
Add the nuts to a frying pan and heat on a very low heat.
Once lightly toasted, remove from the heat and add the Worcestershire sauce and black truffle and stir to fully combine.

To serve:

On a small plate, add the macadamia nuts in a circle and create a ring smaller than the diameter of the tuile with a gap in the middle.
Spoon in some of the parmesan and black truffle sauce.
Gently place the tuile over the top and serve.

Prawn & Toasted Rice Consomme

450ml prawn shell and head stock
1g white pepper
Juice ½ lemon
50ml Noilly Prat

150g prawns
1 shallot
50g toasted rice
Pinch of salt

2 egg whites

Consomme

Start by making the stock.
Add the prawn shells and heads to a pan and gently heat until you can smell the oils. Add the pepper, lemon juice, and Noilly Prat and simmer for 1 minute.
Add 450 mL of water and allow to boil for 15 minutes gently. Check the taste and then pass through a sieve, reserving the stock.

With the prawns, shallots, and toasted rice, add to a blender and blitz to a mousse.

In a separate bowl, whisk the egg whites until just turning foamy.
Mix the egg whites plus the salt into the prawn mousse.
Add the stock from the first part to a heavy-bottomed saucepan and whisk in the egg mixture.
Place this over a gentle heat and simmer. Please do not allow this to boil, and gently stir so it doesn't stick to the bottom.
The egg whites will start coagulating and forming a raft on the surface.
Carefully make a small hole in this raft and agitate the bottom of the pan so all solids rise to the top.

At this stage, taste the consommé and add a little salt if needed.

When the raft is solid, remove the pan from the heat and carefully ladle out the liquid and strain over a muslin lined sieve. Do not press the liquid through, allow it to strain slowly.

Chill the consommé and remove any fat that forms on the surface.

Warm gently before serving.

Prawn

2 whole prawn
Oil

Add the oil to a pan and bring up to a medium heat.

Cook the prawns until slightly charred. Rest and season before serving.

To serve:

Crème fraiche
Finely chopped chives
A few slices of carrot julienne
1 tsp crispy rice

To make the crispy rice, bring a small pan of oil up to about 180 degrees and then drop in the rice.

After about 5 seconds remove the rice and drain. Season very lightly.

In a shallow bowl, spoon in some consommé and add the prawn to the centre of the bowl.
Add some crème fraiche and top this with the fine slices of carrot.
Sprinkle over some chives and finish with the crispy rice.

Grilled Octopus & Fava Puree

Octopus tentacle, 1 per serving

150g yellow split peas (or fava beans)
Water to rinse
Oil
1 shallot
1 tsp cumin, ground
1 tbsp lemon juice
Any leftover jelly from the octopus packaging
Pinch salt
Pinch sugar
300ml water

Octopus

Pat the tentacle dry and in a frying over a low/medium heat with a little oil. Gently cook until cooked through and slightly charred. Remove and lightly season before serving.

Fava puree

Rinse and soak the yellow split peas in line with the packet instructions.
When the yellow split peas are ready, place a medium saucepan over a low heat. Add the shallots and allow to colour slightly for a few minutes.
Add the cumin, lemon juice, jelly, salt, and sugar and cook for 1 minute.
Add the water and yellow split peas and bring to a simmer.
Allow to simmer for 45 minutes and then remove from the heat to cool slightly.
Blitz all of the ingredients until smooth; add a little olive oil if required to achieve the correct consistency (a bit like hummus). Pass through a sieve for a super smooth finish.
Check the taste and add salt and/or lemon juice as required.

1 leek, washed
Oil
Salt
50 ml sunflower oil

Burnt leek puree and leek oil
Preheat the oven to 180 degrees.
Slice the leek lengthways and brush with a little oil and salt.
Cook in the oven until well blackened, and then blitz until smooth. Pass through a sieve.
Spoon into a piping bag.
With the pulp left in the sieve, add this to a small sauce pan with the sunflower oil.
Bring slowly to a simmer and then remove from the heat and allow to infuse for 30 minutes. Pass this through a muslin-lined sieve and reserve the oil.

To serve:

Crispy onion
Mayonnaise

On each of the suckers on the tentacle, alternate dots of leek puree and mayonnaise.
Spoon some of the fava puree onto a plate and drizzle over some of the leek oil.
Carefully top with the octopus tentacle.
Finish by sprinkling on some crispy onions.

Black Malloreddus Carbonara

50g semol flour
25g water
1tsp charcoal powder

Per serving:

Malloreddus (or Sardinian gnocchi)

Mix the black powder with the water and then combine with the flour until fully incorporated.
Knead for 5 minutes until the dough is smooth. Wrap in cling film and allow to rest for 30 minutes.

When ready, divide the dough into 25g pieces and roll out into a thin sausage about 1 cm thick. Cut the sausage shape into 1 cm pieces.

On a gnocchi board, place a piece of dough and press it down and pull it along with a dough scraper so the dough curls up with ridges all around. Place onto a drying tray.

When ready, cook the pasta in salted water for about 3-4 minutes.

30g pancetta
15g grated Parmesan
1/4 clove garlic
1 tsp lemon juice
1 egg yolk
1 anchovy fillet
1 tsp chopped parsley
1 tsp Worcestershire sauce
1 tbsp toasted panko breadcrumbs
Charcoal powder

Salt
Black pepper
1 Romaine lettuce leaf, finely shredded
1 anchovy fillet
Parmesan shavings

Carbonara dressing

Finely dice the pancetta and then cook in a hot frying pan to render all the fat.
In a bowl, add the cheese, garlic, lemon juice, and egg yolk. Mix to a paste.
Mix in the anchovy and parsley and stir to combine.
Add the Worcestershire sauce and the panko breadcrumbs, and then stir through the charcoal powder and mix well. Add some pasta water to loosen as needed.

Add the egg yolk mixture to the pan with the pancetta and stir over a low heat. Add a little more pasta water if needed.

To finish

Add the cooked pasta to the sauce and stir through.
Add the salt and pepper and check the taste.
Add the pasta to a bowl and top with some of the lettuce, an anchovy fillet and some parmesan shavings.

Ham & Cambridge Sauce

Ham hock

3 hard boiled eggs, yolks only
1 tbsp oil, sunflower
2 anchovy fillets
1 tsp capers
1 tbsp chervil, tarragon and chives (finely chopped and mixed)
1 tsp mustard
50ml oil
1 tsp lemon juice
Pinch of caynenne
½ tsp chopped parsley

Parsley, roughly chopped

Ham

Pre heat the oven to 180 degrees.
Cook the ham hock for 40 minutes and then remove and allow to cool.

Cambridge sauce

Mix the egg yolks with sunflower oil.
With a pestle and mortar, grind together the egg yolk mixture with the anchovies, capers, herb mix, and mustard. Once fully combined, transfer this to a bowl.
Gradually add the oil and whisk continuously, and allow the oil to emulsify with the egg mixture.
Finish with the lemon juice, cayenne pepper, and parsley.

To serve:

Slice the ham into thin slices and add to a small plate.
Spoon some of the sauce alongside and sprinkle some parsley over.

Mackerel on Toast

Brioche

250g plain flour
5g salt
3g instant yeast
25g sugar
140ml warm water
1 small egg, about 35g
45g milk
2 tbsp butter, melted

In a bowl, whisk together the flour, salt, yeast, and sugar.
In another bowl, whisk together the water, egg, milk, and butter.
Pour the egg mixture into the flour mixture and bring together with a spatula to form a sticky dough.
Cover the bowl and let rise for 3 hours until doubled in size.
Turn the dough out onto a well-floured surface, shape it into a rough ball, and place it into a floured bowl. Leave to rise for 45 minutes.
Transfer to a spring oven (see crusty bread recipe) and cook for 25 minutes at 220 degrees with the lid on, then 12 minutes with the lid off at 200 degrees.
Remove and allow to cool on a wire rack.
Cut a piece of the brioche loaf into a neat triangle and lightly toast the brioche on all sides in a pan with some salted butter.

Mackerel fillet

1 mackerel fillet
Oil
Salt

In a frying pan, add some oil, then gently fry the mackerel until cooked, and the skin is colored. Remove, drain, and portion into neat pieces on the diagonal, about 3 cm in width. Season lightly.

Mackerel dressing

1 mackerel fillet
20g kombu
75ml sunflower oil
100g soy sauce
½ lemon
25g mirin

Soak the kombu in cold water for 12 hours. Wrap the kombu around the mackerel to cure for 2 days.
After 2 days, chop the mackerel and cook in a pan with the sunflower oil over a low heat.
When the mackerel is cooked, add the soy sauce and bring to a boil.
Pass through a sieve and discard the mackerel; place the reserved oil and soy sauce into the freezer until completely frozen, and then separate the oil from the soy sauce.
Grill the half of the lemon and then squeeze the lemon juice plus the mirin into the infused (and now thawed) soy sauce.
Finish with a dash of the reserved oil (also now thawed) and stir. Check the taste.

To finish:

Parsley, finely chopped

Add the cooked mackerel to the brioche and drizzle over some dressing.
Top with some parsley and serve on a small plate.

Scotch Egg & Chilli Crack

1 egg
Water
Ice water

Boiled egg

Bring a pan of water to the boil.
Weigh the egg and cook in boiling water for exactly 1 minute and 5 seconds per 10 grams.
Remove the egg and place in the ice water.
When fully cooled, peel the egg.

100g pork sausage meat
1 tsp chilli powder
1 tsp garlic salt
1 tbsp cornflour
2 tbsp flour
1 egg, beaten
40g panko breadcrumbs
Rendered pork fat or vegetable oil

Scotch' casing

Mix the sausage meat with the chilli powder and garlic salt until fully combined.
Flatten out the sausage meat into a circle.
Coat the boiled egg in a little cornflour.
Place the boiled egg from above into the middle, and then carefully encase the egg in the sausage meat.
Lightly flour one hand and then roll the scotch egg in the flour.
Next, dredge through the egg and let any excess drip off.
Finally, coat well in panko breadcrumbs, ready for deep frying.
Heat the fat or oil in a small saucepan, deep enough to cover the scotch egg, up to 180 degrees.
Carefully drop in the scotch egg and fry for 4 minutes, turning as needed to ensure an even cook. Remove and allow to drain.

Chilli crack or chilli oil
Sweet chilli sauce

To serve

Liberally brush the outside of the scotch egg in chilli crack and then slice in half and serve immediately alongside some sweet chilli sauce.

Roast Chicken & Truffle Sandwich

Roast chicken

1 chicken breast
Salt
1 tbsp butter
1 tbsp truffle oil
Grated black truffle

Preheat the oven to 180 degrees.
Lightly season the chicken.
Add the butter to an ovenproof frying pan over a low heat.
Fry the chicken breast until slightly browned on both sides.
Add to the oven and cook for around 15 minutes until cooked through.
Remove and allow to cool. Add the truffle oil to the pan, and baste the chicken regularly while it cools.
Once cooled, slice as thinly as possible and grate over some black truffle.

Truffle bechamel

10g butter
10g flour
90g milk
20g cheddar
Grated black truffle
Salt
Black pepper

In a pan, melt the butter, then add the flour and whisk for a couple of minutes.
Gradually add the milk while continuing to whisk until thickened.
Grate in the cheddar, followed by a generous amount of grated black truffle.
Add some salt and black pepper, and then check the taste.
Cover the bechamel until ready to use.

3 slices of bread, thinly sliced
1 tbsp butter, extra for buttering bread
Grated black truffle

To make and finish

Lay a slice of bread and spread it over some of the bechamel.
Top with a layer of the chicken and place another piece of bread on top—butter the middle slice on both sides.
Repeat the layering with bechamel and chicken, then top with the third piece of bread.
Press the sandwich down and the seal in a vacuum bag; place in the fridge for a couple of hours.
Add the butter to a frying pan and melt over medium heat when ready.
Carefully add the sandwich, allow it to toast, and then turn it over to toast the other side.
Remove, drain, and slice as desired.
Finish with a bit of grated truffle and serve warm.

Tuna Tartare & Fennel Seed Cracker

Tuna

80g tuna sashimi
½ shallot, finely chopped
10ml olive oil
0.7g salt

Dice the tuna into even cubes and add to a bowl.
Add the shallot, olive oil and salt to the tuna and gently mix until fully combined.

Egg mayo

1 egg yolk
1 tsp Dijon mustard
Pinch salt
Pinch white pepper
125ml sunflower oil
1 tsp lemon juice
1 egg, hard boiled and roughly chopped

In a bowl, whisk together the egg yolk with the mustard, salt, and pepper.
While continuously whisking, add the oil a drop at a time to start with, whisking until fully combined.
Gradually and slowly add more oil, whisking all the time.
To finish, whisk in the lemon juice and then stir through the boiled egg.

1 tbsp black pepper
2 tbsp fennel seeds
120g flour
Pinch salt
1 egg, separated
60ml milk
25ml olive oil

Micro herbs

Fennel seed crackers

Grind together the pepper and fennel seeds.
Preheat the oven to 190 degrees and line a baking tray with parchment paper.
In a bowl, mix together the flour, pepper, fennel seeds, and salt, then add the egg yolk, milk, and olive oil. The dough shouldn't be too wet but should hold together.
Roll out the dough until very thin and cut to the desired shape.
Lightly whisk the egg white, then brush very lightly over the crackers. Sprinkle over some fennel seeds.
Bake in the oven for around 16 minutes until golden brown and crispy.

To finish:

Add the tuna to a shallow bowl and top with some egg mayo and micro herbs. Serve the crackers alongside.

Basque Style Chorizo Croquettes

Makes about 10 croquettes

260ml whole milk
80ml double cream
35g finely sliced cooked chorizo
25g butter
¼ shallot, finely diced
125g flour
Pinch salt
50g Iberico (or Serrano) ham, finely chopped
1 egg
75g bread crumbs
Oil, for frying

In a saucepan, combine the milk, cream, and chorizo and bring to a simmer over medium heat.
Remove from the heat and leave to infuse for 15 minutes.
In a large sauté pan, melt the butter. Add the shallot and cook until translucent and very tender, about 15 minutes. Add 1/3 of the flour and whisk for 1 minute.
While whisking, add the milk/cream mixture, a little at first, until it is incorporated. Add the salt and check the taste.
Mix the ham into the bechamel and chill for 1 hour either in a roasting tin or a piping bag.
Set out the remaining flour, the egg, beaten, and the breadcrumbs in 3 bowls.
Form a ball of the croquette mix and dredge in the flour, then dip in the egg and finally roll in the breadcrumbs.
In a pan, heat about 5 cm of oil and heat to 180 degrees.
Carefully fry the croquettes in batches until golden brown, turning as they cook to ensure they cook evenly.
When ready, remove and drain and sprinkle with salt.
Serve warm with mayo, aioli, and/or crispy leeks.

Aubergine, Ginger & Rye Bread

Aubergine

1 aubergine
15g brie
1 tsp sumac
Oil
Salt
Pepper

Preheat the oven to 180 degrees.
Slice the aubergine in half lengthways and score the flesh. Season with salt and place face down for 20 minutes then gently wipe away any excess moisture.
In an oven proof frying pan, add some oil and then fry the aubergine, flesh side down, until slightly charred.
Season the aubergine again and then place in the oven for 15 minutes, skin side down.
Remove from the oven and allow to cool slightly.
Remove the flesh from the skin and finely dice.
Stir through the brie and sumac and mix until fully combined. Place in a bowl until ready to serve.

Dukkah

1 tbsp hazelnuts
1 tsp almonds
1 tsp white sesame seeds
1 tsp shelled pistachios
Pinch ground cumin
Pinch ground coriander
Pinch cayenne pepper
Pinch salt

In a frying pan lightly toast the hazelnuts, almonds and sesame seeds.
Add to a blitzer with the remaining ingredients and pulse until coarse.
Store in an airtight container until ready to use.

Ginger beer glaze

90ml ginger beer
75g sugar
25ml sake
60g mirin
50g koji
50g miso
1cm grated ginger

Add all the ingredients to a pan and whisk well to combine.
Heat the pan and bring to a rapid boil for 4 minutes, whisking all the time until the mixture thickens slightly.
Store in a squeezy bottle.

Rye bread

5g active dry yeast
12g honey
150g lukewarm water
4g salt
250g dark rye flour

Add the yeast and about 30 g of water to a bowl, stir, and wait for 5 minutes.
Add in all the remaining ingredients and briefly combine until the mixture is shaggy.
Allow the dough to rest for around 90 minutes, and then bring it together to form a loaf. Rest again for 15 minutes while the oven heats up.
Preheat the oven to 220 degrees and prepare a spring or Dutch oven.
When ready, add the shaped loaf to the spring oven and cook for 25 minutes with the lid on, then remove the lid for another 10 minutes, reducing the oven to 200 degrees.
Remove and allow to cool before slicing thinly.

Micro herbs
Powdered nori

To finish:

Spoon a good amount of the aubergine into a bowl.
Put some of the glaze around the aubergine.
Sprinkle on some of the nori, followed by a good amount of the dukkah and finished with some micro herbs.
Serve a couple of slices of the rye bread alongside.

Wild Garlic Pesto Flatbread

200g '00' flour
130ml warm water
2.6g dry/instant yeast
6g salt
2 tbsp tomato passata
20g grated Parmesan

Flatbread

In a bowl, mix together the water and yeast and leave for 5 minutes.
Add the flour and the salt and mix until combined.
Knead the dough for 6 minutes until smooth.
Leave to rest for 2 hours and then knock back and shape into a ball.
To make the flatbread, flour the work surface and then push out the dough into a circle and stretch by lifting and turning.
Cook on a hot barbecue on one side.
Once nicely charred, turn over and spoon on the passata and sprinkle over the Parmesan.
Place back on the barbecue until the bottom of the bread is charred and the cheese has melted.
While hot, slice into 8 pieces and finish with the pesto, see below.

Pesto

25g wild garlic
45ml olive oil
15g almonds
10g shelled pistachios
35g Parmesan
1/4 garlic clove, blanched
Juice from 1/2 lemon
1g salt
Black pepper

Combine all the ingredients and blitz until very smooth. Loosen with warm water if necessary. Check the taste.
Pass through a sieve into a squeezy bottle.

Crab Crumpet & Mango

100g strong bread flour
50g plain flour
60ml hot water
½ tsp sugar
120ml milk
½ tsp salt
1 tsp bicarbonate of soda (plus 1 tbsp water)
2 tsp dry yeast

100g white crab meat
½ tsp cayenne pepper
½ tsp ground nutmeg
½ tsp paprika
1 tsp lemon zest
1 tsp crab oil
½ tsp salt

Crumpets

Whisk together the sugar, milk, yeast, and hot water and rest for 15 minutes.
In a separate bowl, mix the flour and the salt.
Stir the yeast mixture into the flour and then rest for 2 hours; the mixture should be bubbly.
Mix the bicarbonate of soda with 1 tablespoon of water and stir into the crumpet mixture. Allow to rest for 30 minutes.
Grease a pan with a little oil and butter and a pastry ring with butter, and then add a small ladle of the crumpet mix into the pastry ring in the pan.
Cook slowly over a low heat until set and then carefully flip and cook briefly on the other side until fully cooked through.
Remove and repeat the process with the remaining batter.
Keep the crumpets warm until needed.

Crab

In a bowl, combine all the ingredients and mix well.

Mango

50g diced mango
1 tsp sugar
1 tsp salt
2 tsp white wine vinegar
5g coriander stalks

Take half of the mango and set to one side; they will be used as they are.
For the second half of the mango, add to a small bowl with sugar, salt, white wine vinegar, and coriander stalks and mix well. Leave for 20 minutes and then drain the mango and place on a kitchen towel to soak up any excess liquid.
Place in a clean bowl until needed.

Chilli sauce

¼ red chilli
10ml water
Pinch of salt
40ml white wine vinegar
70g sugar
5g fish sauce
1 tsp grated ginger
1 tbsp cornflour
1 tbsp mango juice

In a small sauce pan, add all the ingredients except the cornflour and mango juice and bring to a boil, stirring all the time.
In a bowl, mix together the cornflour and mango juice and then stir through the sauce. Remove the pan from the heat and allow to cool and thicken.

To finish:

Coriander, roughly chopped, small

Take one crumpet and spoon on some of the crab meat.
Add the mango and the pickled mango and then drizzle over a little chilli sauce.
Finish with a sprinkling of coriander and then serve on a small plate.

Potato Pave

700g Maris piper potatoes
1 sprig rosemary
125ml double cream
1 tbsp butter, finely diced

Potato pave

Preheat the oven to 180 degrees.
Line a small baking tray with parchment paper and allow all sides to overhang.
Peel the potatoes and wash.
Using a mandolin, big peeler, or knife, cut the potatoes as thinly as possible.
Finely chop the rosemary.
Line the prepared tray with 2 layers of potato, 1/3 of the cream, 1/3 of the butter, and 1/3 of the rosemary.
Repeat this twice more and finish with 2 layers of potatoes.
Fold over the baking paper and seal with foil.
Bake for 1 hour; the potato should be tender when a small knife is inserted.
Uncover and cook for a further 30 minutes until golden.
Fold the baking paper back over and place a heavy object on top to press the potatoes.
Place in the fridge overnight to set.
When ready to use the next day, preheat the oven to 200 degrees.
Remove the potato from the fridge, uncover, and take the compressed potato out of the baking tray.
Neatly cut into rectangles of about 8 cm x 3 cm.

Place the slices, cut side up, onto a baking tray and bake for 10 minutes.
Turn over and cook for a further 10 minutes, until golden.

Crème fraiche

100g crème fraiche
1 tsp cornflour

Mix together the crème fraiche and cornflour until fully combined.
Whisk the mixture until thickened and place in a piping bag ready to serve.

To finish:

Salt
Lemon zest
Finely chopped chives
Ground pink peppercorns
Lemon and pepper pearls (Christine le Tennier 'flavor pearls')

Take one piece of potato pave and sprinkle over a little salt.
Top with some crème fraiche.
Add some lemon zest, chives and pink peppercorns.
Finish with a generous teaspoon of the lemon and pepper pearls.

Brandade & Sourdough

180g plain flour
20g spelt flour
126ml water (1)
10ml water (2)
3.6g salt
40g sourdough starter, 100% hydration (at around 24 degrees)

Sourdough

Mix together the flours, the water (1) and the starter until fully combined and leave for 30 minutes.

Add the salt and the water (2) and mix to combine. Knead the dough briefly and then leave to rest for 3 hours in a warm spot.

After 3 hours, fold the dough back in on itself lengthways and then from the sides a couple of times; repeat this 3 more times every 15 minutes.

After the final folds, divide the dough into 6 and shape into small loaves. Rest for 2 hours.

Preheat the oven to 200 degrees. When ready, place the dough in small metal loaf tins and cook for 18 minutes or until golden on top.

Alternatively, 1 large loaf can be made or small rolls.

Once cooked, remove from the tins and allow to cool for 30 minutes before slicing. Per serving, only 1 loaf is required.

When ready to serve, slice a loaf and toast gently in a pan with hot oil.

Brandade

1 cod fillet, approx. 200g
300ml olive oil
1g salt

150g potatoes, peeled and diced
25ml olive oil
2g salt
Juice from ½ a lemon
Parsley, julienned
Chives, finely chopped

Place the cod, the 300 ml olive oil, and the salt into a sauce pan and gently poach for 10 minutes.
Remove the cod and drain it on a piece of kitchen paper.
Gently flake the cod apart, trying to retain the flakes in tact as much as possible.
In another pan, add the potatoes and some water and bring to a boil until.
Drain the potatoes and add the 25 ml of olive oil, salt, lemon juice, parsley, and chives and mash the potatoes.
Carefully fold the cod flakes through the potatoes. Keep warm.

Chicken skin crisps

Skin from 1 chicken breast
Salt
Pepper

Preheat the oven to 180 degrees.
Line a baking tray with parchment paper and place chicken skin on it. Remove any flesh from the skin and stretch the skin out on the tray.
Season the skin with salt and pepper.
Place another piece of parchment paper on top and press down with another baking tray.

Cook for 30 minutes and then remove the top baking tray and parchment paper; place back in the oven until crispy and golden, 5 minutes or so.

When ready, remove from the oven and allow to cool.

Roughly break up the skin into about 3-4 cm pieces.

To finish and serve:

Chopped parsley
Chopped chives
Lemon zest

Take a piece of the toasted sourdough and top with a good spoonful of the brandade. Place the chicken skin into the brandade and then sprinkle over the parsley, chives and lemon zest.

Foie Royale & Brioche

Brioche

250g plain flour
5g salt
3g instant yeast
25g sugar
140ml warm water
1 small egg, about 35g
45g milk
2 tbsp butter, melted

In a bowl, whisk together the flour, salt, yeast, and sugar.
In another bowl, whisk together the water, egg, milk, and butter.
Pour the egg mixture into the flour mixture and bring together with a spatula to form a sticky dough.
Cover the bowl and let rise for 3 hours until doubled in size.
Turn the dough out onto a floured surface, shape it into eight balls, and leave to rise for 45 minutes.
Transfer to a spring oven (see crusty bread recipe) and cook for 22 minutes with the lid on, then 10 minutes with the lid off.
Remove and allow to cool on a wire rack.
Serve as whole rolls or slice as you wish.

Foie Royale

Classic duck foie royale block, about 50g
20g butter
Pinch salt
1 tbsp red wine jelly, see below

Add all the ingredients to a bowl and mix with a fork until fully combined.
Place into a piping bag.

Red wine jelly

185ml red wine
100g sugar
1 star anise
1 clove
2cm piece cinnamon stick
Pinch of allspice
½ vanilla pod
1 orange segment

Place all the ingredients into a pan and heat gently to dissolve the sugar.
Turn up the heat slightly and bring to a boil and then simmer for 15 minutes until the mixture is thick.
Pass through a sieve into a sterilized jar and allow to cool completely.
To serve, place in a piping bag, if required.

To serve

Pipe some of the foie royale butter onto a plate and press with the back of teaspoon.
Fill the indentation with red wine jelly.
Place a sliced brioche roll alongside.

Chicken Katsu Bao

530g flour
2.5g salt
7g dry yeast
40g sugar
15g baking powder
50ml milk
200ml warm water
25ml beef or pork fat

Bao buns

In a bowl, mix together the dry ingredients. Mix the wet ingredients in a separate bowl and then slowly add to the dry ingredients, mixing all the time.
Continue kneading the dough for 5 minutes; it should feel smooth and a little tacky.
Once ready, dust the dough with a little flour and coat with 1 tablespoon of vegetable oil.
Place into a bowl and cover with a damp cloth for around 90 minutes or until doubled in size.
Portion the dough into roughly 50g balls and rest for a few minutes.
Roll out each ball into an oval shape.
Brush a chopstick with oil and then place in the centre of the oval shape; fold the dough over and remove the chopstick.
Place the bao bun onto a piece of parchment paper.
Repeat until all the dough is used and rest for another 30-60 minutes.
When ready, steam the bao buns in a steamer for 8 minutes in batches.
Carefully prise open when ready to fill.

Chicken

2 chicken breasts, cut into strips about 8cm x 2cm
150ml water
15g salt
1 garlic clove, crushed
Oil

Place the water and salt into a bowl and mix well.
Add the garlic and the chicken and cover and place in the fridge for 1 hour.
Remove, rinse and dry the chicken
Heat the oil in a pan and cook the chicken pieces until slightly golden and cooked through.

Katsu

Oil
20g ginger
20g onion
20g garlic
1 carrot
Pinch coriander seeds
Pinch cumin seeds
1 tsp curry powder
½ tsp garam masala
1 tbsp mirin
2 tbsp soy sauce
1 tsp tomato puree
1 tbsp brown sugar
350ml chicken stock
Cornflour and water

Heat the oil in a pan. Add the ginger, onion, garlic, and carrot and cook for 4 minutes.
Add the coriander seeds, cumin seeds, curry powder, and garam masala and cook for 1 minute more.
Add the mirin, soy sauce, tomato puree, brown sugar, and chicken stock and bring to a boil.
Simmer for 20 minutes, then blitz and pass through a sieve.
Weigh the sauce and add to a pan with 7% cornflour, loosened with water, and bring to a boil, whisking slowly until the sauce has thickened to a ketchup consistency.

Panko crumb

50g butter
35g panko breadcrumbs

In a pan, melt the butter until foaming. Add the breadcrumbs and cook until golden.
To remove the breadcrumbs, use a wooden spoon to press them up against the side of the pan to squeeze out any excess butter and place on kitchen paper to drain.

To serve:

Coriander, finely chopped
Black sesame seeds
Carrots, sliced to very thin matchsticks
Spring onions, sliced to very thin matchsticks

Add a little sauce to the bottom of the open bao bun.
Take a piece of chicken and coat well in the breadcrumbs.
Add the chicken to the bao bun and top with some more katsu sauce.
Add some of the carrots and spring onions.
Sprinkle over some, panko, coriander and black sesame seeds to finish.

Grilled Octopus & Fava Puree

Octopus tentacle, 1 per serving

Octopus

Pat the tentacle dry and in a frying over a low medium heat with a little oil. Gently cook until cooked through and slightly charred. Remove and lightly season before serving.

~~100~~ 150 g yellow split peas (or fava beans)
Water to cover
Oil
1 shallot
1 tsp cumin, ground
1 tbsp lemon juice
Any leftover jelly from the octopus packaging
Pinch salt
Pinch sugar
~~20~~ 250 ml water

Greek fava puree

Rinse and soak the yellow split peas in line with the packet instructions.
When the yellow split peas are ready, place a medium saucepan over a low heat. Add the shallots and allow to colour slightly for a few minutes.
Add the cumin, lemon juice, jelly, salt and sugar and cook for 1 minute.
Add the water and yellow split peas and bring to a simmer.
Allow to simmer for 45 minutes and then remove from the heat to cool slightly. Remove some of the liquid and reserve.
Blitz all of the ingredients until smooth; add some of the reserved liquid a little at a time if required to achieve the correct consistency (a bit like hummus). Pass through a sieve for a super smooth finish.
Check the taste and add salt and/or lemon juice as required.

1 leek, washed
Oil
Salt
~50 ml sunflower oil

Burnt leek puree and leek oil

Preheat the oven to 180 degrees.
Slice the leek lengthways and brush with a little oil and salt.
Cook in the oven until well blackened and then blitz until smooth. Pass through a sieve.
Spoon into a piping bag.

Mains & Big Stuff

Wood Pigeon & Autumn Vegetables

Venison & Cauliflower Cheese

Singapore Style Chilli Crab

Lamb, Aubergine & Feta

Lemon Chicken

Cod & Coriander Veloute

Short Rib Pappadelle & Tomato Sauce

Ballotine of Pheasant

Pork, Prunes & Onion Soubise

Lamb Burger

Steak, Miso & Mushroom

Risotto of Squash & Gorgonzola

Sea Bass & Peanut Sauce

Monkfish Vadouvan

Beef, Tamari & Shiitake

Beef & Basil Meatballs

Sage & Bacon Ravioli

Tuna, Gooseberry & Mayo

Lamb, Spiced Red Pepper & Potatoes

Wagyu, Sesame Hollandaise & Nori

Gnocchi Parisienne

Duck & Squash

Pork Belly & Onion Veloute

Salmon & Rose Beurre 'Blanc'

Monkfish, Pork & Black Garlic

Monkfish Curry & Cauliflower

Wagyu Lasagna & Sauce Buccaneer

Inman Ramen

Wood Pigeon & Autumn Vegetables

Wood pigeon breast
Wood pigeon leg
Oil
Salt

Pigeon

Gently panfry the pigeon on the crown and then remove the breast, portion, and keep warm in the oven. The breast should be 68 degrees. Season lightly before serving.

Add the pigeon leg to a small ovenproof dish and cover with oil. Pre-heat the oven to 90 degrees and cook the pigeon leg for 90 minutes. Remove from the oven, remove the leg from the oil, and drain. Season lightly before serving.

1 potato, about 120g
50g Jerusalem artichoke, peeled
Bacon, thinly diced
5g salt
Sprig of thyme
Rosemary, about ½ tsp
1 tbsp butter

Jerusalem artichoke rosti

Grate the potato and artichoke and squeeze out all the liquid; leave in a sieve until ready to use.
Pan fry the bacon and drain any excess fat. Finely chop the bacon and add to the potato mixture along with the salt and herbs.
Form the mixture into small patties of the desired shape and pan fry in the butter until crispy on both sides.

Celeriac puree

Celeriac, half
100 ml milk
1g salt
Pinch cayenne pepper
1 tbsp butter
½ tsp Xanthan gum
1 tsp lemon juice

Peel and roughly chop half a celeriac.
Add the celeriac to a pan with the milk and cook until the celeriac is soft.
Drain the celeriac and blitz with the salt, cayenne pepper, butter, xanthan gum and lemon juice until smooth.

Pigeon sauce

Wood pigeon trimmings
1 tsp allspice
12 blueberries
12 juniper berries
Thyme
Rosemary
30ml balsamic vinegar
30ml white wine vinegar
300ml chicken stock
1 tsp butter
Salt
Lemon juice, drop as required

In the pan used for the pigeon breast, add any trimmings along with the allspice, blueberries, and juniper. Cook for around 5 minutes. Add the thyme and rosemary.
Add the vinegar and reduce by 2/3.
Add the stock and reduce by 2/3.
Pass the sauce through a sieve and return to a pan. Add the butter. Check the taste and adjust accordingly with salt and/or lemon juice.

Cavolo Nero

Cavolo Nero, 1 leaf, stalk removed

Trim a couple of leaves and remove the stalk.
Blanch in salted boiling water for about 2 minutes and then drain.

Beetroot

Beetroot powder

Peel and finely slice a beetroot and place on baking tray. Cook at 120 degrees until dehydrated and crispy. Remove from the oven, allow to cool and then blitz in a spice grinder to a fine powder.

Beetroot ketchup

100g beetroot
25g sugar
25ml rice vinegar
Pinch Xanthan gum

Add all the ingredients to a blitzer and blitz until smooth; place in a piping bag.

To serve:

On a plate, sprinkle over some of the beetroot powder.
Place the pigeon breast and leg on to the plate.
Add the cavolo nero, the rosti, some celeriac puree and beetroot ketchup.
Finish by spooning some of the sauce on and around the pigeon.

Venison & Cauliflower Cheese

Venison

Fillet of venison, about 180g per portion
Salt
Pepper
Oil
1 tbsp butter

Bring the venison up to room temperature and then season all over with salt and pepper.
Pre heat the oven to 180 degrees.
Heat a little oil in a pan and the sear the venison. Add the butter and baste.
Finish in the oven for about 6 minutes and then remove and rest (keep the pan). Slice and season before serving.

Sauce

1 shallot, finely sliced
1 garlic clove, crushed
Thyme
Rosemary
5 black peppercorns
50ml red wine
15ml red wine vinegar
200ml veal stock
1 tbsp butter
Salt
Lemon juice

In the venison pan, gently cook the shallot, garlic, rosemary, thyme, and peppercorns for a few minutes. Add the red wine and red wine vinegar and reduce to syrup.
Add the stock and reduce by about half, and the sauce has thickened. Pass through a sieve.
Finish the sauce with the butter, and then check the taste. If necessary, adjust with salt and a drop of lemon juice.

Cauliflower cheese

80g cauliflower florets, any thick stalks removed
10g butter
10g flour
110g milk
0.5g salt
Pinch white pepper
Pinch grated nutmeg
25g cheese (cheddar, mozzarella, Parmesan or Comte, or a combination)
10g grated Parmesan
15g panko breadcrumbs, toasted
15g crispy onions
Chives, finely chopped
Micro greens

Preheat the oven to 180 degrees.
Boil the cauliflower in a sauce pan of salted water until softened.
Melt the butter in a separate pan, then stir through the flour to make a roux.
Gradually add the milk and whisk continually to combine until all the milk is added and the sauce has thickened.
Add the salt, pepper and nutmeg and then stir through the cheese until the cheese is fully melted.
Add the cauliflower to a small oven-proof dish and spoon over the sauce.
Top with the grated Parmesan and bake for 20 minutes.
Remove from the oven and allow to rest for 4 minutes, then sprinkle over the toasted breadcrumbs, the crispy onions, the chives and micro greens.

Roast potatoes

1 Maris piper per serving, peeled, rinsed and chopped into 4 equal pieces
Salt
Duck fat, 2 tbsp
Garlic, 1 clove, crushed
Rosemary, 1 sprig

In a sauce pan, add water, salt and potatoes and bring to a simmer.
Boil until the potatoes are very soft but still retaining their shape.
Drain and allow to cool.
Pre heat the oven to 180 degrees.
Add some duck fat to a small roasting tray and put in the oven.

Once the fat is hot add the potatoes and roast for around 1 hour.
After 40 minutes, add the garlic and the rosemary and a little salt and give the potatoes a shake. Cook for a little longer until the potatoes are golden and crispy. Season before serving.

Yorkshire pudding

Beef fat
1 large free range egg
50g flour
50g milk
Salt, pinch
Pepper, pinch

Pre heat the oven to 225 degrees.
In a cupcake tray or Yorkshire pudding tin, add a little beef fat to 6 compartments. Put this in the oven for 20 minutes.
In a bowl, beat the eggs, flour, milk, salt and pepper until smooth.
Remove the tray from the oven and then carefully pour in the batter evenly.
Put the tray back into the oven and cook for 14 minutes until well risen, golden and crispy.

To serve:

Chopped parsley

Add the sliced venison to a plate
Place some cauliflower cheese and roast potatoes alongside.
Sprinkle over some parsley then top with a Yorkshire pudding.
Spoon some sauce over the venison and potatoes or serve alongside.

Singapore Style Chilli Crab

Crab

Cooked crab claws, about 5-6
1 tbsp crab chilli oil

Lightly crack the claws and brush them liberally with the oil.

Sauce

2 red chillis, finely chopped
1cm grated ginger
1 garlic clove, grated
200ml dashi
1 tbsp honey
30g sugar
1 tbsp chilli crab oil

IIn a pan, heat the chili, ginger, garlic, dashi, honey, sugar and oil and whisk while it heats up. Allow it to boil for a couple of minutes and then leave it to cool slightly. This is the chili stock.

75ml chilli stock
2 tbsp crab chili oil
1 tbsp rice vinegar
1 tbsp soy sauce
1 tsp tomato paste
1 tsp cornflour/water
Few drops lemon juice

Add the crab chili oil, rice vinegar, soy sauce and tomato paste to a separate pan and heat gently for 1 minute.
Add the chili stock and stir to combine.
Add the cornflour/water and stir until thickened. Check the taste and add the lemon juice as needed.
Just before serving, stir the crab meat through the sauce.

Rice (per serving)

30g rice
1 tsp sugar
1 tsp red wine vinegar
½ tsp salt

Cook the rice according to the instructions. Once cooked, stir through the sugar, red wine vinegar and salt.

Deep fried bun

125g T55 flour (or 110g plain flour, 15g cornflour)
3g salt
20g sugar
60g water
10g rapeseed oil
3.6g yeast
1 tbsp crab chilli oil

Mix all ingredients except the crab chili oil until smooth. Knead for a couple of minutes. Place in the fridge for as long as possible.

Portion the dough into 40 g each and roll into neat balls.

Remove the dough from the refrigerator and rest at room temperature until the balls have doubled.

Heat the oven to 100 degrees, stream bake the buns for 12 minutes, then turn the oven off. Please wait 8 minutes before taking them out of the oven.

Heat oil in a pan to 190 degrees. Deep fry the buns until golden brown and then remove and drain. Brush with a bit of crab chili oil before serving.

Spring onions, green part, finely chopped
Coriander, roughly chopped

To serve:

Add the rice to a bowl and top with the crab and sauce.
Spoon over some extra sauce.
Sprinkle over some spring onion and coriander.
Slice a deep fried bun in half and serve on a separate plate alongside.

Lamb, Aubergine & Feta

Lamb, for two portions

Lamb rack
1 tbsp oil
1 tbsp butter
1 tbsp black sesame seeds
1 tbsp finely chopped pistachios
1 tbsp breadcrumbs

Preheat the oven to 200 degrees. In a frying pan, add the oil and sear the lamb for one minute on the rounded side. Baste while searing. Turn the lamb over, add the butter, and sear for another minute while basting. Place the lamb in the oven for 4 minutes; turn over and cook for another 4 minutes. Remove from the oven, cover in foil, and rest for 4 minutes.
Blitz the sesame seeds, chopped pistachios, and breadcrumbs.
Remove the foil after 4 minutes, brush with a little oil, and cover with the breadcrumbs. Place under a grill for 1 minute, but do not burn. Carve.

Tomato powder

Skins from 2 tomatoes

Dehydrate the skins in the oven at 90 degrees for about 45 minutes or until completely dry.
Finely chop the skins once cooled or blitz to a powder.

Basil ketchup:

50ml rice wine vinegar
30g sugar
30g blanched basil leaves
½ tsp xanthan gum

Once the basil leaves have been drained, reserve the water.
Blitz all of the ingredients together - if it's too thick, add some reserved water, if it's too thin, add a another pinch of xanthan gum.
Place into a bottle or piping bag.

Aubergine:

1 medium aubergine
400g chopped tomatoes
1 garlic clove, sliced into 6 pieces lengthways
Olive oil
1 small white onion, finely diced
Cracked black pepper
1 tsp cumin
1 tsp ground coriander
½ tsp ground cardomom
Pinch of sugar
1 tsp grated ginger
Salt
3 basil leaves
30g crumbled feta

Slice the aubergine lengthways, season well and leave for 20 minutes to extract the bitterness. Pat off any excess liquid.
Score the aubergine with a knife in a criss cross pattern and insert the sliced garlic into some of the scored lines.
Add a little oil to a hot frying pan and add the aubergine, flesh side down and cook until slightly blackened.
Drizzle with a little more oil then place in the oven until well charred. Remove and allow to cool.
Whilst the aubergine is roasting, gently fry the diced onion in a little oil.
When it is softened, add some black pepper and the spices plus the sugar.

Stir until well combined and then stir through the tomatoes. Grate in the ginger and stir through.

Remove the aubergine flesh from the skin and finely chop. Add the aubergine to the pan with the onion and tomato and gently heat through until the mixture comes together and most of liquid has been cooked off. Check the taste and add a little salt and pepper if need be.

When ready to serve, sprinkle over the feta and basil.

To serve:

Sprinkle the plate with tomato powder. Spoon the aubergine and tomato onto the plate and arrange the lamb alongside. Dot some basil ketchup around the lamb.

Lemon Chicken

1 chicken breast, cut into roughly 3cm cubes

Marinade:
½ lemon zest
1 garlic clove, crushed
1 tbsp soy sauce
Pinch of salt
1 tbsp lemon juice
Pinch of sugar

Breading:
50g plain flour
1 beaten egg
50g panko breadcrumbs
Oil for frying
Black and white sesame seeds

Chicken

Mix together the marinade ingredients and then add the cubed chicken.
Allow to marinade for 2 hours

Remove the chicken from the marinade and then coat in flour, dip in the egg and then coat in breadcrumbs.

Heat the oil in a small saucepan and then deep fry the chicken in a couple of batches until golden.
Remove drain and sprinkle over the sesame seeds.

100ml chicken stock
½ lemon zest
Juice from 1 lemon
4 tbsp sugar
1 tbsp water / 1 tbsp cornflour

Sauce

In a saucepan, heat and reduce the chicken stock by about 2/3. In a bowl, whisk together the zest, juice, and sugar, and then add to the reduced stock and stir through. Combine the water and corn flour, and then add to the sauce over a low heat and stir through for about 5 minutes. Check the taste.

25g white rice, cooked as per the packet instructions
1 tsp lemon juice
Pinch sugar
Pinch salt
1 tsp red wine vinegar

25g plain flour
25g rye flour
Pinch chinese five spice
Pinch of salt
1 tbsp olive oil
35ml water
1 tbsp sesame seeds
1 tbsp coriander seeds
1 tbsp fennel seeds

Sliced spring onions
Sesame seeds (black and white)

Rice:

Once the rice is cooked, season it with the lemon juice, sugar, salt and red wine vinegar and stir to fully combine.

Chinese cracker:

Mix the flour, salt, and five spices, then add the water and oil and bring together roughly until a dough forms.
Do not knead.
Tip out the dough and cut into 4 equal pieces. Roll it out as thinly as possible and shape it into the desired shape. Brush with oil, prick well with a fork, and sprinkle over the seeds.
Line a baking tray with baking paper and bake for around 9 minutes at 180 degrees or until golden and evenly cooked (and crispy).

To serve:

Add the rice to a bowl or plate and top wth the chicken. Spoon over the sauce and then finish with the chopped spring onions and a little more sesame seeds.
Serve the crackers alongside.

Cod & Coriander Veloute

Pan fried cod

Piece of cod loin
200ml water
20g salt
Oil
1 tbsp butter
Lemon juice

In a shallow bowl, add the water and salt and mix well.
Add the cod, cover, and place in the fridge for 23 minutes.
Remove from the fridge and then remove the cod, rinse, and pat dry.
Heat the oil in a pan and then gently fry the cod.
Just before finishing cooking, add the butter and lemon juice and baste the fish.
Remove the cod and allow to rest in the butter and lemon juice.

Pistachio crust

25g pistachios
Oil, for brushing

Blitz the pistachios into a crumb and lay out on a tray.
Just before serving, brush the oil over the top of the rested cod.
Dip the oiled side of the cod into the pistachios and then remove, ready to serve.

Coriander velouté

25g coriander
5g mint
5g parsley
100ml chicken stock
10ml double cream
1 tsp lemon juice
0.5g salt
1 tsp butter

In a pan of boiling water, drop in the herbs and quickly remove and place in ice water. Combine the herbs and chicken stock and blitz until smooth. Pass through a fine sieve. In a small sauce pan, heat the mixture and then stir through the cream, lemon juice, and salt.
Keep warm and finish with the butter.

Coriander oil

25g coriander
50ml rapeseed oil

Add the coriander and oil to a small saucepan. Heat gently for about 5 minutes and then leave to cool and infuse.
Once cooled, blitz the oil and then pass through a sieve.

Cucumber matchsticks

Cucumber
15ml white wine vinegar
Lime juice, from 1 lime
5g sugar
5g salt
5g coriander stalks
Lime zest
Micro herbs

Chop the cucumber into about 8 cm pieces and then chop into matchsticks.
In a small bowl, mix all the other ingredients except the lime zest and then add the cucumber matchsticks.
After about 20 minutes, remove the cucumber and drain carefully on a piece of kitchen paper and mix with the micro herbs. Sprinkle over the lime zest.

1 large potato, Maris Piper
Salt
Oil
Salt
Nori powder (toasted and blitzed nori)

Potato tubes

Peel the potato, and then, with an apple corer, make potato cylinders.
Boil the potatoes in salted water until softened, and then drain.
Preheat the oven to 180 degrees.
Add the oil to a baking tray and then place the tray into the oven.
Once the oil is hot, add the potatoes, coat in the hot oil, and then roast for 45 minutes, shaking occasionally. Season just before finishing cooking.
Remove from the oven when golden, and then sprinkle over the nori powder.

To serve

Add the cod to the plate and spoon around some of the velouté.
Dot some oil around the veloute
Neatly arrange the pickled cucumber and micro herbs as a side salad.
Place the potato tubes alongside the cod.

Short Rib Pappadelle & Tomato Sauce

85g 00 flour
15g semolina
1 egg
1 egg yolk

Pappadelle

Mix the flours and create a well in the middle.
Add the egg and egg yolk and mix together until thoroughly combined.
Once the dough has come together, knead well for about 8 minutes and then leave to rest in the fridge for 30 minutes.
Remove the dough from the fridge and roll out on a lightly floured surface as thin as possible (it's best to use a pasta machine with the second thinnest setting).
Cut the pasta into 1 cm strips and then cover until ready to cook.
To cook, bring some well-salted water to a boil and then add the pasta and cook for 2 minutes.
Drain and serve.

Braised short rib

400g short rib
200ml red wine
200ml water
35ml soy sauce
20g kombu
1 tsb bonito flakes
25ml rice vinegar
15ml mirin
15ml sake
15g brown sugar
5g tomato puree
1 carrot, roughly chopped
1 shallot, roughly chopped
1 garlic clove crushed
Parsley, about 5g

Apart from the red wine and water, blitz together all the other ingredients and marinade the short rib for at least 4 hours. Preheat the oven to 120 degrees.

Once marinaded, add the short rib and marinade to a baking dish, and then add the red wine and water (add a little more water if needed to cover the meat).

Cover the dish in foil and cook for 4 hours. Once cooked, remove from the oven and remove the short rib from the liquid. Wrap the short rib in cling film and place in the fridge under a press.

Pass the liquid through a muslin-lined sieve and retain (see below).

When ready to serve, remove the short rib from the fridge and portion into neat squares or rectangles. Fry off gently in a frying pan before serving.

Tomato sauce

1 tomato
1 tsp butter
1 tsp flour
Red wine stock (see above, roughly 150ml)
Salt, as needed
Lemon juice, as needed

Preheat the oven to 180 degrees.
Place the tomato in the oven and cook until slightly blackened, roughly 20 minutes.
Once cooked, remove the tomato from the oven and place in a sauce pan with the butter and flour. Bring up to a medium heat while stirring until a roux is formed, then add the stock and stir to combine. Allow the mixture to reduce by about 2/3, then pass through a sieve.
Check the taste and adjust with a little salt and/or lemon juice as needed.

To serve:

Parsley, roughly chopped

Add the pasta to a shallow bowl.
Add the short rib and finish with some chopped parsley.

Ballotine of Pheasant

1 shallot, finely diced
1 tsp oil
Small pinch of cinnamon
Small pinch of coriander
Small pinch of cumin
¼ quince
Juice of ¼ lemon
1 tbsp butter
25g chestnut puree
2 pheasant breasts
3 rashers streaky bacon

Pheasant

Start by grating the quince and quickly adding the lemon juice to prevent browning. In a pan, heat the oil and cook the shallot until soft.
Add the spices, quince, and butter and cook for around 5 minutes.
Add the chestnut puree, stir through, and then place in a bowl and allow to cool.
Open up each pheasant breast by slicing out the mini fillet and laying flat.
Spoon the cooled shallot mixture down the middle of one breast and then top with the second breast, placing the wider end of the second one over the narrow end of the bottom one.
Lay out bacon on a work surface and then place the stuffed pheasant breasts on top.
Roll up the bacon around the pheasant and wrap tightly in cling film and tie the ends.
Place in the fridge and allow to firm up for an hour at least.
Preheat the oven to 200 degrees.
When ready, remove the cling film and cook the ballotine in an ovenproof frying pan until coloured all around.
Place into the oven for 10 minutes.
Remove and wrap in foil until ready to serve.
Keep the pan for the sauce.

Sauce

25ml sherry vinegar
100g chicken stock plus pheasant bones
1 tbsp quince jelly
1 tsp butter
Pinch of salt

In the pan used to cook the pheasant, place it back over a medium heat and add the sherry vinegar to glaze the pan.

Add the chicken stock and any pheasant bones and trimmings and reduce by about 2/3.

Stir through the quince jelly and then finish with the butter and salt.

Celeriac puree

Celeriac, half, peeled and diced
Water, to cover
Salt
1 tbsp butter
1 tbsp cream
Pinch of salt
Pinch of white pepper
Drop of lemon juice
Black truffle

In a pan, add the celery, water, and salt and bring to a boil. Boil until the celeriac is softened.

Drain and reserve some of the cooking water.

Blitz the celeriac with the butter, cream, salt, and white pepper until smooth and creamy.

Add some of the reserved cooking liquid if need be until the desired consistency is achieved.

Add a drop of lemon juice and check the taste.

Before serving, grate over some black truffle.

Brussels sprouts, shredded
2 tbsp butter
Salt
1 tbsp orange juice
Zest ¼ orange
Black truffle

Brussels sprouts

Add the shredded sprouts to a small frying pan with half of the butter and heat gently.
Cook until the sprouts are soft, and then add the salt, orange juice, zest, and the remaining butter.
Fry for a couple of minutes until the sprouts are nicely glazed.
Thinly slice the black truffle and top the sprouts with a few slices.

To serve

Spoon some celeriac puree onto the plate and then add the sliced pheasant.
Add some sprouts alongside, and then spoon on some sauce.

Pork, Prunes & Onion Soubise

400g pork shoulder
1 carrot, roughly chopped
1 onion, roughly chopped
2 sprigs rosemary
100ml white wine
300ml water
5 black peppercorns
Apple peel, see below

Pork

Place all the ingredients except the pork into a deep baking tray.
Add the pork, skin side up, and add more water if need be so that all the meat is submerged.
Cook for 90 minutes and then remove and allow to rest.
Strain the cooking liquid (and reserve for use as a stock in another recipe).
Once rested, slice the pork into about 1 cm slices.

2 prunes per serving

Prunes

Finely chop the prunes.

1 Granny Smith apple, peeled and diced to about 1cm (use peels for the pork cooking liquid, see above)
1 tsp sugar
25ml water

Apple

Add all the ingredients to a pan and heat gently and allow to simmer.
Cook for about 5 minutes, until the apple has softened but retains its shape.
Drain the apples from the cooking liquid.

Onion soubise

10g butter
10g flour
120ml milk
Salt
White pepper
2 white onions finely chopped, plus extra butter, about 1 tbsp
1 tsp cream
1 tsp miso paste
Lemon juice

Start by making a bechamel; melt the butter in a pan, then add the flour.
Cook for a few minutes, then gradually add the milk while whisking until thickened.
Allow to cook for a few more minutes, then season with salt and white pepper. Cover and keep warm.
In a separate pan, add the extra butter and the onions and sauté until soft.
Once softened, blitz the onions with the cream, miso, and a couple of drops of lemon juice until a smooth puree is achieved.
Stir the onion puree into the bechamel until fully combined.

Crispy potatoes

1 tbsp potato airbag per serving
Oil for deep frying

Heat the oil to about 180 degrees.
Drop in the potato airbag and allow it to crisp up (about 15 seconds).
Remove and drain. Lightly season.

2 tbsp salt
4 sage leaves
2 thyme sprigs

Herb salt

Cover a bowl with cling film and place the sage and thyme on top.
Microwave for 60 seconds, or until crispy, by cooking in further 10 second increments.
Place the dried herbs into a bowl with the salt and crush to a fine salt.

To serve:

Start by adding 2 or 3 slices of the pork with some crackling to a shallow plate. Add some apple and prunes to the pork and then spoon over some onion soubise. Finish with the crispy potato and herb salt.

Lamb Burger

125g T55 flour (or 110g plain flour, 15g cornflour)
3g salt
20g sugar
60g water
10g rapeseed oil
3.6g yeast
Charcoal powder or black food colouring
1 tsp oil
Sesame seeds

Steamed bun

In a small bowl, combine the yeast, sugar, and water and mix well.
Leave for a few minutes until foamy.
In a separate bowl, combine the flour, salt, oil, and charcoal powder.
Add the yeast mixture to the flour and mix until smooth.
Knead for a couple of minutes.
Place in a bowl and cover for 1 hour.
Portion the dough into roughly 75g each and roll into neat balls. Rest for 30 minutes.
Heat the oven up to 100 degrees and steam bake the buns for 12 minutes, then turn the oven off. Wait 8 minutes before taking them out of the oven.
Brush with the oil and sprinkle over the sesame seeds before serving.

Burger

Per burger:

125g lamb mince
15ml Shaoxing rice wine
15ml soy sauce
15g sugar
1 spring onion, finely sliced
1 tsp orange zest
Pinch of crushed Sichuan peppercorns

Mix together all of the ingredients in a bowl and then form into a patty and allow to rest for a few minutes before cooking. Heat a frying pan and add a little oil. Gently fry the burger on both sides until fully cooked through.

Fillings and accompaniments

15g coriander, roughly chopped
Baby gem lettuce, shredded
1 shallot, thinly sliced
1 tbsp salt
1 tbsp sugar
1 tbsp rice wine vinegar
25g pomegranate seeds
Pinch chilli flakes

In a small bowl, add the salt, sugar and rice wine vinegar and mix well. Add the shallots and leave to pickle for 15 minutes; drain. Combine the coriander, lettuce and pickled shallots. Gently stir through the pomegranate seeds and the chilli flakes. Add to a small salad bowl.

Sauce

½ tsp sesame oil
3 tbsp peanut butter
1 tsp rice wine vinegar
1 tsp soy sauce
Pinch of sugar
Pinch of salt
Pinch of white pepper

Mix together all of the ingredients to form the sauce.

To serve

Slice the bun in half and add some sauce to the base.
Add the burger next and top with a handful of the salad (fillings and accompaniments).
Add the top part of the burger bun and press down slightly.
Place the bun onto a plate and add some salad alongside with some extra sauce, if desired.

Steak, Miso & Mushroom

200g steak, per serving
Salt
Pepper
Oil
Garlic, crushed
2 tbsp butter
1 tbsp miso

Steak and miso butter

Start by mixing the butter and miso together until fully combined, and then shape into a cylinder.
Season the steak with salt and pepper.
Heat some oil in a pan. Add the steak and cook on both sides to achieve the desired finish; after turning, add the garlic.
When resting, add half of the miso butter to the steak and baste while it rests.
Just before serving, slice the steak and add the remaining butter.

2 maitake 'hen of the woods' mushrooms
1 piece kombu
1 shallot, diced
90g plain flour
30g cornflour
1/2 tsp baking powder
1/2 tsp garlic powder
1/2 tsp paprika
Oil for frying

Mushrooms

Break the mushroom into bite size pieces.
In a sauce pan, add the kombu, shallots and salt and bring to a simmer.
Add the mushrooms to the simmering liquid and poach for around 5 minutes - do not boil.
Remove the mushrooms and drain in a sieve.
In a bowl, mix the flours, baking powder, garlic powder and paprika.
In another bowl, add the beaten egg.

Add the drained mushrooms to the flour mixture to coat and then dust off any excess; place into the egg and then transfer back to the flour mixture. Ensure the mushroom pieces are evenly coated. Remove and shake off any excess flour. Heat the oil in a saucepan to around 180 degrees, and then deep fry the mushrooms for about 5 minutes or until brown and crispy. Remove and drain, and then season.

Lime zest
Micro herbs

To serve:

Place the steak on a plate, topped with a disc of the miso butter.
Add the deep-fried mushroom pieces. Sprinkle some lime zest over the mushrooms and the micro herbs over the whole dish.

(The mushrooms could be served on their own as a small plate with extra lime zest and a lime mayo as a dip on the side.)

Risotto of Squash & Gorgonzola

Rice

30g risotto rice
150ml water
0.53g salt

In a pan, add the rice, salt and water and cook until nearly fully done.
Drain and reserve the rice.

'Acid' butter

15g butter
½ shallot
3 black peppercorns
2 tbsp white wine vinegar
2 tbsp white wine
2 sage leaves

In a pan, add the butter and heat gently until melted.
Add all the other ingredients and bring to a boil.
Allow to reduce until almost all the liquid has gone and then pass through a sieve, discarding the solids and keeping the melted butter.

Risotto

1 tbsp grated gorgonzola
1 tsp Parmesan
1 tbsp mascarpone
Acid butter from above, about 1 tbsp
Rice from above

Add the rice back into a pan and stir through the butter, gorgonzola, Parmesan and mascarpone over a low heat until fully combined.

Squash

½ butternut squash
Oil, for deep frying
15ml white wine vinegar
15ml water
3 black peppercorns
1 sage leaf

First, make some crisps by finely slicing some of the squash and then deep-frying in oil at 180 degrees. Remove, drain, and season ready to serve.

For the pickled squash, finely dice some of the squash and then add to a bowl with the white wine vinegar, water, peppercorns, and sage. Allow to pickle for 18 minutes and then drain.

Sage

15g sage
30g butter
½ clove garlic, grated
Few drops of lemon juice
Oil for deep frying

Reserve 3 sage leaves.
Add the remaining sage to a small pan with the butter, garlic, and lemon juice and gently heat while stirring.
Once the butter has melted, remove from the heat, pass through a sieve, and then serve immediately.
With the reserved sage leaves, deep fry in oil at 180 degrees for a few seconds until crispy. Drain and season lightly.

Pine nuts, lightly toasted and roughly chopped
Grated parmesan
Crumbled gorgonzola
Lemon zest
Micro herbs

To serve:

Add the risotto to a shallow bowl, and spoon in some of the sage butter.
Top with the pickled squash, squash crisps, and sage crisps.
Finish with a sprinkle of pine nuts, the grated parmesan and gorgonzola, and some lemon zest. If using, finish with a few micro herbs.

Sea Bass & Peanut Sauce

1 sea bass fillet, cut in half
Oil, for brushing
50g peanut butter
½ red red chilli
1 tsp sesame oil
1 shallot
1 tsp mirin
1 tsp rice vinegar
2 tsp soy sauce
1 tbsp brown sugar
60ml water

1 tbsp chopped, toasted peanuts
½ tsp mild chilli powder or flakes
1 tbsp sesame seeds, white and black
Pinch of sugar
Pinch of salt
1 tbsp nori powder

Sea bass and peanut sauce

Start by making the sauce.
Add the peanut butter, red chilli, sesame oil, shallot, mirin, rice vinegar, soy sauce, and brown sugar to a pan. Add the water, bring to a boil, and simmer for 5 minutes. Remove from the heat and then blitz until smooth.
Remove the skin from the sea bass and brush with a little oil.
Lay out a piece of cling film and place one piece of sea bass. Spoon some of the sauce on top of the sea bass and then place the second piece on top.
Wrap the sea bass in the cling film.
Set up a steamer and then steam the sea bass for 9 minutes.
Remove, allow to cool slightly, and then remove the cling film ready to serve.

Furikake crumb

Mix all of the ingredients together in a bowl. until fully combine

Leftover peanut sauce from above
1 tbsp cream
Chips, seasoned with nori powder, or a bit of leftover furikake

To serve:

Gently heat any leftover sauce and let down with a little bit of cream, up to 1 tbsp, and stir to combine.
Gently spoon some of the furikake over the sea bass and then add to a plate.
Spoon on some of the sauce next to the sea bass and then finish with some chips or serve the chips alongside.

Monkfish Vadouvan

Monkfish

Monkfish fillet
Butter
1 tsp crispy onion
1 tsp onion powder
1 tsp coriander seeds
1 tsp salt
1 tsp turmeric
½ tsp fenugreek
½ tsp cumin powder
½ tsp black pepper
½ tsp chilli powder
½ tsp garlic powder
½ tsp ginger powder
½ tsp caraway seeds

Start by making the vadouvan spice mix. Add all of the ingredients except the fish and butter to a pestle and mortar and crush together.
Use the spice mix to coat the monkfish on all sides. Reserve a little spice mix, see below.
Heat a frying pan and add the butter. Add the monkfish and cook gently to achieve a crust on all sides.
Remove and allow to rest, basting with any pan juices.

Squash puree

Butternut squash, flesh only - skin and seeds removed
Water
Salt, 1 tsp
1 tbsp cream
Vadouvan spice mix from above (about ½ - 1 tsp)

Add the squash to a pan with enough water to cover and the salt.
Bring to a boil and allow to simmer until the squash is cooked and falls off a knife when inserted.
Drain the squash and reserve some water. Add the cream and the spice mix to the squash and blitz until smooth; add a little of the reserved water if need be to achieve the right consistency. Check the taste and season if required.

Peas

50g peas, frozen
½ shallot, finely chopped

Cook the peas in boiling water and then drain.
Gently fry the shallots until cooked but not coloured.
Stir the shallots through the peas and keep warm, ready to serve.

Onion rings

½ shallot, cut into rings
30ml beer
50ml water
50g flour
10g cornflour
1 tsp turmeric
Oil for deep frying

Mix together the beer, water, flour, and turmeric and stir until smooth.
Heat the oil to about 160 degrees in a pan.
Dredge the shallot rings through the batter and then fry until crispy.
Remove and drain.

To serve:

Slice the monkfish into neat portions.
Spoon some squash into the middle of the plate and add the monkfish slightly to one side.
Add the peas and shallots alongside.
Top the fish with the shallot rings.

Beef, Tamari & Shiitake

1 small fillet of beef, about 180g
25ml tamari
50g shiitake mushrooms, finely sliced
50ml apple juice
½ onion, finely chopped
1 sprig rosemary

Beef

In a small sauce pan, add the tamari and mushrooms and bring to a simmer. Cook for 5 minutes and then remove from the heat and allow to infuse for 10 minutes.
Strain the liquid and brush liberally over the beef.
In another pan, add the apple juice, onion, and rosemary and bring to a boil. Allow to reduce until a syrupy consistency.
Cook the beef in a pan, basting with the tamari glaze occasionally. Once cooked as desired, remove the beef from the pan and brush with a little of the apple syrup while it rests.
Reserve some of the tamari glaze and apple syrup for the sauce; see below.

Tamari glaze from above
Apple syrup, from above
½ chopped onion
1 sprig rosemary
1/2 onion, chopped
Shiitake stock (100g mushrooms, 200ml boiling water)
Charcoal powder
Rice vinegar
1 tsp butter

Sauce

Add the tamari glaze, apple syrup, rosemary, and onion to a pan and cook gently for a couple of minutes.
Add the stock and bring to a boil. Continue cooking until reduced by about ¾. Pass through a sieve.
Add a little charcoal powder to achieve a black sauce.
Check the taste and adjust with a little rice vinegar. Stir through the butter to finish.

Salad

1 lettuce leaf
Ginger, finely chopped into strands
¼ red chilli

Finely chop the lettuce leaf and combine with the ginger.
Finely slice the red chilli and add to the lettuce and ginger.
Arrange neatly to serve.

Potato terrine

250g maris piper potato
100g shiitake mushrooms
30g beef fat
1 sprig rosemary
Salt

Peel the potato slices as finely as possible.
Rinse under cold water, then squeeze out any liquid; drain.
Finely slice the mushrooms.
Melt the beef fat in a small sauce pan with the rosemary.
In a small dish or terrine pan, line with baking paper with plenty of excess over the edges.
Start with a layer of potatoes, brush over the beef fat, add a layer of mushrooms, and then sprinkle with a little salt.
Repeat this layering until the dish is full, finishing with a layer of potato.
Cover the terrine with the excess baking paper and then place it under another dish.
Preheat the oven to 180 degrees.
Cook the terrine for 1 hour and check it's cooked through by inserting a skewer.

Remove from the oven and allow to cool. Place in the fridge under a weight to firm up.
Once fully cooled and pressed, remove the terrine, unwrap it, and carefully portion into neat pieces.

To serve

Parsley, finely chopped

Place the glazed beef onto a plate. Arrange the salad and terrine alongside. Finish by spooning in some sauce to the middle of the plate and sprinkling over some chopped parsley.

Beef & Basil Meatballs

Meatballs

200g beef mince, good quality
1.5g salt
20g finely diced feta
5 basil leaves, very finely chopped
1 egg yolk
15g breadcrumbs

In a bowl, mix all the ingredients until fully combined.
Divide into roughly 30g pieces and then roll into a ball.
Heat the oven to 180 degrees and then cook the meatballs on a small tray lined with baking paper for 12 minutes.
Remove from the oven and finish in a frying pan to brown on all sides.
Drain and keep warm.

Crispy pasta

40g durum or semol flour
20g water

Combine the flour and water and knead for 5 minutes until soft and shiny.
Allow to rest for 5 minutes.
Roll out the dough to the thinnest setting on a pasta machine and then cut into spaghetti, roughly 15cm in length.
Cook in salted, boiling water for 15 minutes and then remove and drain.
Take a few strands of pasta and roll into a small portion; repeat with the rest of the pasta.
Place the rolled pasta onto a grill pan and place under a hot grill until lightly golden; turn over and grill the other side.

Sauce

10g flour
10g butter
5g tomato puree
15g bacon lardons
½ carrot, finely sliced
½ celery stalk, finely sliced
½ onion, finely sliced
2 tomatoes
5 basil leaves
150g vegetable stock
1 piece of kombu
Black pepper
To finish: pinch of salt, 1 tsp butter, couple of drops of lemon juice

In a saucepan, add the butter and flour to form a roux. Add the tomato puree and stir to combine. Remove the red roux and allow to cool.
In the same pan add the lardons, carrot, celery and onion and cook until softened. Add the roux back in along with the tomatoes, basil and stock and stir until fully combined.
Add in the kombu and a little black pepper and bring to a boil. Allow to simmer for around 25 minutes.
Remove from the heat and then blitz.
Pass through a sieve and squeeze out all the sauce.
Check the taste and add the salt, butter and lemon juice.

Salad

Spinach leaves, cut into fine strips
Basil leaves, cut into fine strips
Small amount of lemon zest
Feta, crumbled
Pinch of salt

Mix the spinach and basil and then stir through the lemon zest and feta.
Add a little salt

Extra virgin olive oil
Black pepper

To serve

On a plate or shallow bowl, add the crispy pasta and top with the meatballs.
Spoon over some sauce.
Place a small handful of the salad alongside.
Finish by drizzling over some olive oil and topping with a couple of twists of black pepper.

Sage & Bacon Ravioli

80g bacon
100g ricotta
5 sage leaves, finely chopped
Pinch salt
Black pepper

Filling

In a pan, fry off the bacon until slightly crispy and then drain off the rendered fat and reserve (see below).
Allow the cooked bacon to cool and chop as finely as possible.
Combine ¾ of the chopped bacon with the remaining ingredients and place into a piping bag; reserve the remaining ¼.

120g semol flour
1 egg
1 egg yolk
1 tsp olive oil
Pinch salt

Pasta dough

Mix together all of the ingredients and knead for 5 minutes.
Wrap in cling film and rest for 15 minutes.
Once the filling is prepared, roll out the dough to the thinnest setting on the pasta machine to cut into 2 equal rectangular pieces.
Place a good amount of the filling about 10cm apart on one of the pasta sheets and brush the edges with water.
Place the second pasta sheet on top and gently press down around the filling.
Cut the pasta around the filling into the desired shape and place on a floured tray.
Cook in salted water for about 3 minutes, then drain and serve.

Sauce

Bacon fat, reserved from above
1 tbsp butter
1 tsp lemon juice
¼ garlic clove, grated
Chopped bacon, from above
1 tbsp grated parmesan
5 sage leaves, roughly chopped
Salt
Black pepper

In a pan, reheat the bacon fat and then add the butter, lemon juice, garlic and bacon and stir to combine.
Add the parmesan and sage and stir through.
Finish the sauce with some salt and pepper.

To finish

Add the ravioli to a pasta dish and then spoon over a generous amount of the sauce.

Tuna, Gooseberry & Mayo

Tuna

120g tuna sashimi

Slice three pieces of tuna very thin and put to one side.
With the remaining tuna, cut into even squares.
Just before serving, gently sear the sides of the tuna squares in a hot pan. Season lightly.

Gooseberry relish

100g diced gooseberry
30g sugar
1 tsp tomato puree
2 tbsp rice vinegar
1 tsp salt
1 tsp ground coriander
1 tbsp water

Add all the ingredients to a pan and bring to a simmer. Leave to simmer with the lid on for 10 minutes and then allow to cool.

Accompaniments

Radish
Micro herbs
Mayo & wasabi paste
Crispy rice
Nori

Finely slice the radish into even circles.
Cut some micro herbs, about 1 tbsp.
Mix the mayo and wasabi paste and place into a piping bag.
Crisp up some rice in hot oil; drain and lightly season.
Cut some nori into rectangles about ½ cm x 2 cm.

Sushi rice

60g sushi rice
1 piece kombu
150ml water
1 tsp red wine vinegar
Drop sesame oil
1 tsp sugar
1 tsp salt

Rinse the rice in cold water until the water runs clear.
Add the rice plus the water to a small pan with the kombu and bring to a boil. Cover and allow to simmer until all the water has been absorbed and the rice is tender.
In another pan, heat the red wine vinegar, sesame oil, sugar, and salt, and then allow to cool.
Once the seasoning has cooled, add it to the rice and stir through until the rice is sticky.
Divide the rice into three equal parts.

To serve:

Decorate a plate with some wasabi mayo, crispy rice, and gooseberry relish.
Place the seared tuna squares onto the plate and dot with some wasabi mayo and gooseberry relish.
Place some micro herbs and crispy rice alongside.
For each portion of sushi rice, squeeze into a rugby ball shape and then top with a slice of tuna. Top the tuna with a piece of radish, a dot of mayo, and a piece of nori.

Lamb, Spiced Red Pepper & Potato

Lamb

1 lamb rump
Salt
½ tsp ground cumin
½ tsp garlic powder
½ tsp lemon zest

In an ovenproof pan, gently cook the lamb rump, skin side down to render the fat.
Once the skin of the lamb is crispy, season the meat with salt. ground cumin, garlic powder and lemon zest.
Vacuum pack the lamb and cook in water bath for 2 hours at 62 degrees (for a medium finish).
Once cooked, allow to rest and then portion neatly.

Spiced red pepper

¼ onion, finely diced
¼ celery, finely diced
¼ carrot, finely diced
¼ garlic clove, crushed
1 tbsp butter
1 tsp tomato paste
2 red peppers, roughly chopped
1 tsp harissa paste

In a pan, cook the onion, celery, carrot and garlic in the butter until softened.
Add the tomato paste and red peppers and cook for 15 minutes. Stir through the harissa paste for the last 5 minutes.
Blitz the mixture until smooth. Check the taste and if necessary, adjust with a little salt and/or lemon juice.

Potatoes

80g new potatoes, per portion
Salt
Water, for boiling
1 tsp honey
1 tsp olive oil
½ tsp harissa paste

In a pan, boil the potatoes in salted water until softened. Remove, drain, and slightly rough up the edges of the potatoes.
Preheat the oven to 180 degrees.
In a small bowl, mix together the honey, oil, and harissa. Combine this with the potatoes and mix well.
Place in the oven for 10 minutes.

To finish:

Add the lamb to the plate and serve the potatoes and the spiced red pepper alongside.

City Glass

Wagyu, Sesame Hollandaise & Nori

Steak (per serving)

180g wagyu steak
30g shio koji

Brine the steak in the shio koji for around 1 hour and then rinse off and pat dry.
Take 3 thin slices of steak and put to one side.
With the remaining steak, cook in a medium/hot pan with oil, removing and slightly resting the steak a couple of times during the cooking process. Once the steak is caramelised on both sides and cooked to your liking, remove and allow to rest, basting in any pan juices.

With the 3 thin slices, briefly cook these over the barbecue and then brush with tare*.

Hollandaise

1 egg yolk
Pinch salt
Pinch white pepper
1 tsp rice vinegar
70g sesame oil (No. 0)
10g miso
Drop mirin

In a bowl, whisk together the egg yolk, salt, pepper, and rice vinegar until light and fluffy.
Place the bowl over a pan of simmering water and keep whisking while gradually adding the sesame oil.
Once fully combined, whisk in the miso. If need be, loosen the mixture with a little lukewarm water.
Check the taste and season with mirin if required.

Broccoli

2 pieces of tenderstem broccoli
Salt

Lightly season the broccoli and dry fry until slightly charred.

Sushi rice

60g sushi rice
1 piece kombu
150ml water
1 tsp red wine vinegar
Drop sesame oil
1 tsp sugar
1 tsp salt

Rinse the rice in cold water until the water runs clear.
Add the rice plus the water to a small pan with the kombu and bring to a boil. Cover and allow to simmer until all the water has been absorbed and the rice is tender.
In another pan, heat the red wine vinegar, sesame oil, sugar, and salt, and then allow to cool.

To serve:

Slice the cooked steak and dust with a little nori powder.
Place the steak on the plate add the broccoli alongside.
Spoon some hollandaise over the broccoli.
Spoon on some sushi rice.

With the remaining sushi rice, squeeze it into 3 small oblong shapes and top with the reserved slices of steak. On top of this, dot some hollandaise, sprinkle over some nori powder, and finish with a small strip of nori. Place on the plate.

Tare: 50 ml sake, 50 ml burnt-off mirin, 55 g sugar, 60 g dashi soy, and 2 g dashi powder. Add all ingredients to a pan and bring to a boil, then store in an airtight container.

Gnocchi Parisienne

50g butter
120g water
120g flour
½ tsp Dijon mustard
2 eggs
30g Parmesan, grated
Salt
Pepper

Gnocchi

In a pan, heat the butter and water until the butter has fully melted.
Next, add in the flour and stir until smooth. Gently cook out the flour, and when ready, the mixture will easily release from the side of the pan. Allow to cool slightly.
Stir in the eggs, one by one, until fully incorporated, followed by the mustard, Parmesan, and salt and pepper. Spoon into a piping bag.

To cook, fill a large saucepan with water and season well.
Tie a piece of string around the pan, with one piece going tightly across the pan.
Bring the water to a boil and then pipe the gnocchi, cutting off 2 cm pieces, into the boiling water.
When the gnocchi floats, it is ready.
Remove and drain on kitchen paper.
See below for final cooking steps.

Sauce

1 tbsp oil
50g asparagus
40g purple sprouting broccoli
Gnocchi from above, cooked
50ml chicken stock
50g butter
1 tsp Dijon mustard
Juice from ½ lemon
1 tsp parsley, roughly chopped
1 tsp mint, roughly chopped
1 tsp tarragon, roughly chopped

In a pan, heat the oil and then add the asparagus, broccoli and gnocchi and heat until slightly coloured.
In another pan, bring the chicken stock to the boil and reduce slightly and then lower the heat.

Stir in the butter, mustard and lemon juice until fully emulsified.
Pour the sauce over the gnocchi and vegetables and then stir through the herbs. Serve in a warm bowl.

Duck & Squash

Duck

Duck breast
Salt
Pepper
Thyme, 2 sprigs
1 garlic clove, crushed

Score the skin of the duck breast and season lightly with salt and pepper.
Add the duck, skin side down, to a pan and then gently cook over a low heat, spooning off the fat as it renders.
Once the skin is crispy, lightly season the flesh side and turn the breast over. Add the thyme and garlic and cook for a further 5 minutes.
Once done, remove from the heat but leave in the pan to continue cooking with the residual heat.
When ready, remove from the pan and slice evenly. Keep the pan, see below.

Sauce

25ml red wine
50ml chicken stock
10ml Madeira
1 tsp thyme leaves
Pinch of salt
1 drop lemon juice
2 tsp butter

In the pan used to cook the duck, add the red wine and deglaze the pan.
Allow the red wine to reduce to almost nothing.
Add the stock and reduce by half or until nicely thickened.
Pass through a sieve and then return to a pan and add the Madeira and thyme leaves and stir to combine.
Add the salt, lemon juice, and butter and whisk together until the butter has melted.

Squash puree

1 butternut squash, peeled and roughly diced
Water
Salt
5 thyme sprigs
½ garlic clove
Pinch of cayenne pepper
1 tsp rice vinegar

In a pan, add the squash and enough water to cover.
Add some salt, the thyme, and the garlic.
Bring to a boil and cook until the squash is soft.
Drain the squash and reserve some of the cooking water.
Remove the thyme, add the cayenne pepper and the rice vinegar, and then blitz until smooth; if need be, loosen with some of the reserved cooking water. Check the taste and adjust if necessary.

Pommes Parmentier

2 maris piper potatoes
30g beef fat
1 piece kombu
1/2 clove garlic, crushed
2 sprigs thyme
Salt

Preheat the oven to 180 degrees.
Add the oil or beef fat to a small roasting tray and place in the oven.
Peel the potatoes and cut into neat rectangles.
Evenly dice the potatoes.
In a pan, add the potatoes with the kombu and cover with water.
Bring to a boil and cook until the potatoes are softened slightly but retain their shape.

Drain the potatoes and add to the roasting tray in the oven along with the garlic, thyme and salt.
Cook for around 30 minutes, shaking occasionally until golden.
Remove and drain on kitchen paper.
Season lightly to finish.

To finish and serve:

Thyme leaves

Spoon some of the squash puree onto a plate.
Add the sliced duck breast followed by the pommes Parmentier.
Sprinkle over some thyme leaves.
Finish with the duck sauce or serve alongside for pouring at the table.

Pork Belly & Onion Veloute

800g pork belly
5 sprigs thyme
1 piece garlic, crushed
1 sprig rosemary

Pork belly skin, from above
1 tsp salt
1 tsp garlic powder
½ tsp celery salt
½ tsp white pepper
½ tsp paprika
¼ tsp turmeric
½ tsp dried parsley
½ tsp dried oregano
½ tsp dried rosemary
½ tsp dried thyme
½ tsp dried tarragon
½ tsp onion powder
½ tsp cayenne pepper

Pork belly

Add all the ingredients to a vacuum pack and seal.
Set up a sous vide machine and water bath and cook the pork belly for 12 hours at 62 degrees.
When finished, remove from the bag and place under a press in the fridge.
When ready to prepare the dish, remove the pork from the fridge. Remove about a 2cm slice of the skin and place to one side, see below.
With the remaining pork belly, cut into neat rectangle portions and then gently fry in a pan with a little oil until the skin is crispy. Remove, rest and keep warm.

Spiced skin

Mix together all of the salt, herbs and spices and crush together in a pestle and mortar.
Dry the pork belly skin and then shallow fry in a little oil until crispy. Remove and drain the skin.
Sprinkle the cooked, crispy skin liberally with the spice mix.

Onion velouté

1 white onion, roughly chopped
1 tbsp oil
200ml vegetable stock
2 tbsp double cream
Salt
Pepper
½ tsp lemon juice
1 tsp thyme leaves

In a pan, add the oil and onion and soften over a low heat.
Add the stock and simmer for around 15 minutes.
Add the onions and stock to a blitzer and add the cream, salt, pepper, lemon juice and thyme leaves.
Blitz until smooth and check the seasoning.
Keep warm.

Potatoes

120g new potatoes
1 tbsp olive oil
Salt
Pinch of the spice mix from above

In a pan, add the potatoes and cover with water and add some salt.
Bring to a boil and cook until the potatoes are softened.
Remove and drain the potatoes and then mix with the olive oil, salt and spice mix.
Serve on the plate or in a side plate alongside.

To serve:

Add a piece of pork belly to the plate.
Spoon some onion velouté alongside and then place the spiced pork skin neatly on the plate.
Serve the potatoes on a small plate alongside.

Salmon & Rose Beurre 'Blanc'

Salmon

160g sashimi grade salmon
Tare (see page XXX)
Nori powder

Carefully slice off 3 thin pieces of salmon and reserve, see below.
Set up a pan and a steamer and cook the salmon for 4 minutes.
Brush the salmon with tare and rest until needed.
Just before serving, gently colour with a blowtorch and then sprinkle over some nori powder.

Beurre 'blanc'

50ml rose wine
25ml white wine vinegar
1 small shallot, finely chopped
2 pink peppercorns
100g butter, cold, diced

Put the wine, vinegar, shallot, and peppercorns into a saucepan and bring to a simmer.
Cook until the liquid has reduced to 2 tbsp and pass through a sieve.
Place 1 tbsp back into the pan over a low heat.
Add the butter, 1 dice at a time, and whisk until fully melted before adding the next dice of butter. Keep the heat low, and if the sauce looks greasy, remove from the heat and keep whisking. Once half of the butter has been added, start adding 2 pieces at a time, whisking continuously, and the sauce should become thick and glossy.
Check the taste and season with some of the reserved reduction if necessary.
Serve immediately.

Sushi rice

60g sushi rice
1 piece kombu
150ml water
1 tsp red wine vinegar
Drop sesame oil
1 tsp sugar
1 tsp salt
Lettuce leaves, cut into 1 inch strips

Rinse the rice in cold water until the water runs clear.
Add the rice plus the water to a small pan with the kombu and bring to a boil. Cover and allow to simmer until all the water has been absorbed and the rice is tender.
In another pan, heat the red wine vinegar, sesame oil, sugar, and salt, and then allow to cool.
Once the seasoning has cooled, add it to the rice and stir through until the rice is sticky.
Divide the rice into three equal parts and wrap in a strip of lettuce.

To serve:

Shredded lettuce
3 slices of salmon from above
Mayonnaise
Nori powder

On the left-hand side of the plate, spoon on some beurre 'blanc' and add the steamed salmon.
Top the salmon with a little shredded lettuce.
On the right-hand side, place the wrapped rice and top each with a slice of salmon. Place a dot of mayo on top and then sprinkle over some nori powder.
Garnish the plate with a little shredded lettuce, if desired.

Monkfish, Pork & Black Garlic

Pork fillet
1 tsp salt
1 tbsp Chinese five spice
Oil
1 tbsp honey

Pork

Pre heat the oven to 180 degrees.
Mix together the salt and five spices.
Rub the pork fillet in the salt mixture.
Heat a little oil in an ovenproof dish and sear the pork until all sides are well coloured. Brush with the honey.
Place the pork into the oven and cook for around 12 minutes or until the internal temperature reaches 62 degrees.
Remove and allow to rest before slicing and serving.

Monkfish fillet
Salt

Monkfish

Season the monkfish and then wrap them in cling film.
Place into a steamer and cook for 12 minutes.
Carefully unwrap and rest the fish before slicing and serving.

Black garlic mash potatoes

200g potatoes, peeled and evenly chopped
4g salt
25g butter
50ml milk
20g black garlic cloves, chopped
2 tsp parley, roughly chopped

Add the potatoes and 3g salt to a saucepan and bring to a boil.
Once softened, drain.
In another pan, heat the butter, milk, 1g salt, and black garlic for 5 minutes and then mash until smooth.
Add the drained potatoes to the butter mixture and mash until smooth.
Keep warm and add the parsley once served on a plate.

Pickled shallots

1 shallot
1 thyme sprig
1 star anise
20ml white wine vinegar
20ml water
1 tsp sugar
½ tsp salt

Peel the shallot and cut it across to achieve shallot rings, and place it in a bowl.
In a small pan, heat all of the other ingredients for a couple of minutes, stirring gently.
Pour the pickling mixture over the shallots and leave for at least 30 minutes.
When ready to serve, remove a few shallot rings. The remaining shallots can be covered and left in the bowl.

1 shallot, peeled and chopped
1/2 tsp sugar
Pinch of five spice powder
25ml red wine
1 tsp soy sauce or umami sauce
100ml chicken stock
1 tsp butter
½ tsp rice wine vinegar
½ tsp mirin

Sauce

In the pan used to cook the pork, add the shallot and cook over medium heat for a couple of minutes until coloured and softened.
Add the sugar and five spices powder to coat the shallots.
Deglaze the pan with the red wine and turn up the heat.
Add the soy sauce.
Reduce the liquid until it has almost completely evaporated.
Add in a ladle of the chicken stock and reduce until thickened.
Add more stock as required and reduce until the sauce is thick and glossy.
Remove the sauce from the heat and pass through a sieve. Finish the sauce with the butter, rice wine vinegar, and mirin. Whisk until fully emulsified and check the taste.

To serve:

Add the slices of pork and monkfish alternately on the plate. Spoon some garlic mash topped with parsley onto the plate. Pour on a little sauce and serve some more alongside. Finish with some of the pickled shallot rings neatly placed onto the plate.

Monkfish Curry & Cauliflower

Curry sauce

10g butter
8g flour
120ml chicken stock
Pinch of salt
1 tbsp cream
1 tbsp S&B curry powder
Pinch ground cumin
Pinch ground ginger
Pinch garam masala

In a pan, melt the butter over a low heat and then whisk in the flour to form roux. Gradually add in the chicken stock, whisking all the time until the sauce has thickened. Add the salt.
Whisk in the cream, curry powder, cumin, ginger, and garam masala.
Check the taste and keep the sauce warm.

Monkfish

1 monkfish fillet
1 tbsp curry powder
1 tsp salt
Oil

Season the monkfish with the salt and coat in the curry powder.
Add the oil to a pan over low to medium heat.
Add the monkfish to the pan and sear on both sides until well charred and fully cooked.
Remove and allow to rest.

Rice

50g jasmine rice per serving
125ml water
1 tsp soy sauce
1 tsp red wine vinegar
½ tsp sesame oil
Pinch of salt
Pinch of garlic powder
Pinch of onion powder
Pinch of ginger powder

Cook the rice in the water (or according to packet instructions) and drain.
In another bowl, add all the other ingredients and mix well.
Pour the seasoning mix from the bowl over the rice and stir well.

Cauliflower

3 cauliflower florets per serving
1 tsp lime juice
25ml olive oil
1 tsp curry powder
Pinch salt
Pinch black pepper
Lime zest

In a small pan, add some water and par boil the cauliflower.
Preheat the oven to 180 degrees.
In a bowl, mix together all the other ingredients and stir well to combine.
Drain the cauliflower and then place it in the bowl with the oil mixture to coat the cauliflower.
Place the cauliflower on a baking tray (pour over any excess liquid) and cook for 20 minutes.
Remove and allow to rest for a few minutes, and add some lime zest before serving.

To finish and serve:

Chopped chives
Wilted spinach
Peanuts, roasted and finely chopped
Coriander, roughly chopped
Lime zest
Spring onion, finely sliced

Start by adding some of the curry sauce to a plate or shallow bowl.
Neatly add and arrange the monkfish, rice, and cauliflower.
Place some chives on the monkfish and some wilted spinach on the cauliflower.
Finish by sprinkling over the peanuts, coriander, lime zest, and spring onion.

Wagyu Lasagna & Sauce Buccaneer

Pasta (1)

60g semol flour
3 egg yolks
Black colouring (4-5 drops to achieve a dark black colour)
Drop of olive oil
Pinch of salt

On a board, tip out the flour and gradually mix in the egg yolks and black colouring.
Add the oil and salt and continue mixing until the dough is uniform black.
Knead the dough for 8 minutes until smooth.
Allow to rest for 30 minutes.
When ready, roll out the dough to around 2 mm.
Dust with a little flour.

Pasta (2)

25g spinach
65g semol flour
1 egg
Drop of olive oil
Pinch of salt

Steam the spinach until wilted, and then remove, lay out, and cool in the fridge.
Once cooled, blitz the spinach with the egg, oil, and salt.
On a board, tip out the flour and mix in the spinach and egg mixture.
Continue mixing until a uniform green colour.
Knead the dough for 8 minutes until smooth.
When ready, roll out the dough to about 2 mm and dust with a little flour.

To finish the pasta, slice the green pasta into 2 cm strips and lay out the green stripes onto the black pasta. Gently roll the green pasta into the black pasta with a rolling pin. Set up a pasta machine and pass the stripy pass through until the thinnest setting. Cut the pasta into rectangles of 7 cm x 12 cm. When ready to cook, bring a pan of salted water to the boil and cook a couple of sheets per portion. Remove and drain ready to serve.

Wagyu mince

Oil
½ onion, finely chopped
¼ carrot, finely chopped
¼ celery stick, finely chopped
1 tsp tomato puree
¼ garlic, crushed
Salt
Black pepper
125g wagyu mince per portion

In a shallow pan, heat the oil and then gently cook the onion, carrot, and celery until softened.
Stir through the tomato puree and the garlic.
Season with a little salt and black pepper.
Add the wagyu mince and continue cooking until just cooked through.
Check the taste; the mince should be fairly dry.
Keep warm until needed.

Buccaneer sauce

55g butter, split into 30g and 25g
1 shallot, finely diced
20g ginger, grated
½ banana (not overly ripe)
3 tbsp raspberry vinegar*
150ml veal stock
Salt
Pepper

In a pan, add 30g butter and melt.
Add the shallot and cook until softened.
Stir through the ginger and banana.
Next, stir in the raspberry vinegar and reduce slightly.
Add the veal stock and reduce by about half until thickened.
Pass through a sieve, check the taste, and then season with salt and pepper as required.
Finish by whisking in the 25g butter, 5g at a time, until fully emulsified.

To finish:

Black truffle, for grating
1 tsp crispy onions

In a pasta bowl or deep plate, add a spoonful of the mince and grate over some black truffles, and add some crispy onions. Spoon over some sauce and then top with a sheet of the cooked pasta.
Repeat the plating on top and finish the dish with a spoonful of sauce.

Inman Ramen

Chicken broth

1kg chicken bones or wings
100g white mushrooms, finely sliced
1 onion, quartered
5g dashi powder

In a stock pot, add the bones, mushrooms, and onion and cover with cold water. Bring to a simmer and cook for 2 hours, removing any scum from the surface. When ready, pass through another sieve into a saucepan and stir in the dashi powder.
Keep warm until needed.

Pork belly

800g pork belly
1 tbsp soy sauce
1 tbsp sake
1 tbsp mirin
1 tbsp sugar
1 clove garlic, crushed
1 spring onion, roughly chopped
Water, as needed

Bring the pork belly up to room temperature and score and season the skin.
Pre heat the oven to 220 degrees.
In a roasting tray, add all the ingredients except the pork belly and mix together. Place the pork belly in the roasting tray and top up with water if necessary so that the liquid is below the level of the skin.
Place the tray into the oven immediately, turn it down to 180 degrees and cook for 1 hour.
Remove the pork from the tray and allow to rest before slicing to serve.
Reserve the cooking liquid, see below.

2 slices bacon
½ tsp dashi powder
100ml reserved pork belly cooking liquid

Ramen noodles
Egg
Enoki mushrooms
Spring onion
Carrot
Sesame seeds, black and white

Bacon tare

Add all the ingredients to a sauce pan and slowly bring to a boil.
Once the bacon is fully cooked, pass through a sieve and reserve the liquid.

Other

Cook the ramen noodles as required.
Boil an egg for 4 minutes and then just before it's time to serve, slice in half.
Gently pan fry some enoki mushrooms until slightly coloured and softened.
Finely slice both the green and white part of a spring onion.
Finely slice the carrot.

To serve:

Add some bacon tare to a ramen bowl.
Top this up with some chicken broth and add the noodles.
On one side of the bowl, add some sliced pork belly.
Place the boiled egg into the middle of the bowl and finish on the right with the mushrooms, spring onions and carrots.
Sprinkle over some sesame seeds to finish.

Desserts & Sweet Stuff

Pecan Ice Cream & Dark Chocolate

Jerusalem Artichoke Fudge

Soho Bun

Scottish Tablet Sundae

Per & Ginger Crumble with Dark Chocolate

Lemon Tart

Amaretto & Ginger Cheesecake

Chocolate & Orange Fondant

Madeleines of Lemon & Thyme

Lime & Mint Panna Cotta

Lemon & Pistachio Financier

London Cheesecake

Shortbread, Jam & Burnt Meringue

Amaretti & Basque Cheesecake

Tarte Bordaloue

Date Cake & Miso Caramel

Fig & Orange Cheesecake

Chocolate & Fig Oat Cookies

Pistachio Cake & Creme Chiboust

Pain Perdu & Chocolate

Cinnamon Cracker & Cheddar

Meringue, Coffee & Autumn Fruits

Crema Catalana

Pistachio Tiramisu

Champagne Truffles

Pineapple & Lime

Pink Pralines

Choux au Craquelin

Chocolate Marquise & Miso Cremeux

Pink Pralines

Lemon Parfait & Meringue

Pecan Ice Cream & Dark Chocolate

Ice cream

200g double cream
200g condensed milk
40g pecan nuts, blitzed
30g coco pops, crushed

Take half of the double cream and whisk until thickened (ribbon stage).
Add half of the condensed milk and stir through.
Add the blitzed pecan nuts and stir to fully combine. Place in a pastry ring in a tub and put into the freezer until set.
Repeat the above but instead of adding the pecans, add the coco pops.

Tuile

90g water
10g flour
30g oil
Pinch salt
1 tsp cocoa powder

Add the flour, oil, salt and cocoa powder to a squeezy bottle and shake until combined. Heat a frying pan and then squeeze in some of the liquid and cook until a tuile forms. Gently remove from the pan and allow to cool.

Caramel

125g sugar
2 tbsp water
70g double cream
25g butter
Pinch salt

Add the sugar and water to sauce pan and heat until a golden caramel forms; leave to go darker if you don't want the overall dish to be too sweet. Remove the pan from the heat and add the cream, butter and salt and stir to fully combine. Store the caramel in a squeezy bottle.

Chopped pecans
Coarse sea salt

Chopped pecans

Finely chop the pecans and mix with some coarse sea salt.

To serve:

On a plate, add the caramel in the required pattern and sprinkle over some salted pecans.
Add the coco pop ice cream to the plate and top with the pecan ice cream.
Add the tuile to the top of the ice creams.

Jerusalem Artichoke Fudge

100g Jerusalem artichokes, peeled
55g butter
100ml whipping cream
125g liquid glucose
5ml cider vinegar
3g salt
50g milk chocolate

Fudge

Roughly chop the artichokes and blitz for a few minutes.
Add the artichokes to a saucepan and reduce to a dark syrup.
Add the glucose, syrup, and cream and slowly bring up to 100 degrees.
Stir the mixture until it reaches 116 degrees, then remove from the heat and beat in the butter.
While still hot, beat in the vinegar and salt.
Line a deep baking tray with parchment paper and pour in the fudge mixture. Once cooled, place in the freezer to set.
Once set, remove and cut into 2 cm squares and place on more parchment.
Melt the chocolate over a Bain Marie and then drip over the fudge squares. Remove any excess chocolate and return to the freezer to allow the chocolate to set.
To serve, remove from the freezer, trim the edges, and leave to thaw in the fridge for 15 minutes.

Soho Bun

Makes 8-10

3.5g dry or instant yeast
20ml whole milk
30g caster sugar
50ml double cream
1 large egg
185g strong white bread flour
Pinch salt
40g butter, diced
30g dark chocolate, chopped into small pieces
30g milk chocolate, chopped into small pieces
30g white chocolate, chopped into small pieces
1 egg yolk, beaten plus pinch of salt

Whisk together the yeast, milk, and ½ teaspoon of the sugar with a fork until thoroughly combined, and leave to rest for 5 minutes. In the bowl of a stand mixer with the dough hook, add the cream, egg, and yeast mixture, followed by the flour and the rest of the sugar. Mix and knead until a sticky dough forms, about 2 minutes. Add the butter in 2 stages plus the salt and knead for 5 minutes. The dough should become shiny and smooth. Add all the chopped chocolates and mix in. Cover the bowl with a tea towel and leave to rest for one hour at room temperature. When ready, flour the work surface and your hands, knock the dough back, and divide into 12 pieces (should be roughly 45-50 g each). Shape into little balls and place on a lined baking tray with gaps between each ball; leave gaps of about 5 cm. Cover the buns again with a cake tin lid that doesn't come into contact with the buns, and leave again for 1 hour. Preheat the oven to 190 degrees. After an hour, glaze the buns with the egg yolk and bake for 16 minutes until golden. Remove from the oven and, while still warm, grate over some dark and white chocolate.

Scottish Tablet Sundae

Ice cream

180g sugar
50ml whole milk
17g softened butter
40g sweetened condensed milk

Whisk the cream until thickened and then add the condensed milk, vanilla and white chocolate and stir until fully combined. Place in the freezer for a few hours.

Caramel

50g sugar
15ml water
10g butter
28ml double cream, room temperature
1 tbsp miso

Melt the sugar with the water in a pan to form a light caramel. Add the butter, cream and miso and stir until fully combined. Remove and pour the miso caramel into a jug.

Tablet

100g double cream
90g condensed milk
Drop of vanilla essence
20g grated white chocolate

Line a tray with baking paper.
Mix together the sugar, butter, and whole milk. Add to a pan with the condensed milk and bring to a boil up to 120 degrees. Then allow to simmer for 10 minutes, stirring continuously. The mixture should darken; remove from the heat and beat until thick. Pour the mixture into the lined tray and allow to set for 2 hours.
Once ready, break into small pieces.

Chocolate popcorn
Squirty cream

To serve:

Take a sundae dish or glass bowl and build as follows:
1. Spoon in some ice cream
2. Pour over some miso caramel sauce
3. Add some chocolate popcorn
4. Add some tablet pieces
5. Repeat steps 1 to 4
6. Add some squirty cream
7. Add some more caramel sauce
8. Top with some more tablet

Pear & Ginger Crumble with Dark Chocolate

Base

12 ginger nut biscuits
60g butter

Crush the biscuits to a fine crumb.
Melt the butter and then mix with the biscuit crumbs.
Spread the mixture across the bottom of a 24 x 16 baking tray lined with baking paper.
Place in the fridge to set.

Pear filling

6 pears, peeled and diced
1 tbsp sugar

In a small pan, add the pears and sugar and over a medium heat, bring the mixture to a simmer and cook until the pears have softened but maintain their shape.
Pour this over the ginger nut base.

Topping

50g oats
25g melted butter
25g brown sugar
1 tsp ground ginger
15g walnuts, roughly chopped
5g grated dark chocolate
Pinch of salt

Pre heat the oven to 180 degrees.
Mix together all of the ingredients until fully combined and then spread evenly over the pear filling.
Place the pear crumble into the oven and bake for 18 minutes.

Pear accompaniment

¼ pear, peeled and trimmed to keep pear shape
150ml ginger ale
1cm grated ginger
Pinch of salt
Grated chocolate

In a small pan, add all the ingredients except the grated chocolate and poach gently until the pear is softened. Once softened, coat in the grated chocolate ready to serve alongside the crumble.

Dark chocolate sauce

75g 70% chocolate
13g butter
63ml double cream
7½ g sugar
12 1/2 g amaretto

Melt the chocolate over a Bain Marie then add the butter, cream and sugar and stir until smooth.
Stir in the amaretto and transfer to a small serving jug.

To serve:

Take a slice of the crumble and add to shallow bowl or plate.
Place the poached pear alongside and finish with some of the chocolate sauce.

Lemon Tart

375g all butter shortcrust pastry
4 unwaxed lemons
170g butter, cubed
5 eggs
1 egg yolk, beaten
220g caster sugar

Creme fraiche
Raspberries

1 tart, 23cm tart tin, plus baking beans
Roll out the pastry between 2 sheets of cling film until 2 mm thick and 33 cm in diameter.
Preheat the oven to 180 degrees.
Carefully take off the cling film and roll the pastry around a rolling pin and place it in the tart tin. The edges will hang over; press the pastry into the tin and prick with a fork. Leave to rest for 45 minutes in the fridge.
Gently trim the edges to neaten up.
Scrunch up a piece of baking paper and lay it over the pastry, and add the baking beans on top.
Bake for 20 minutes.
Remove the paper and baking beans and cook for a further 10 minutes until golden brown.
Remove from the oven and allow to cool completely before tidying the edges with a microplane.
Carefully lift the tart case out of the tin onto a serving plate.

Zest 3 of the lemons and reserve the zest. Roll all 4 lemons on the worktop and then juice and measure out 150 ml.

Place the reserved zest, the 150ml juice plus the butter, eggs, egg yolk, and sugar into a saucepan over a low heat and stir continuously for 12 minutes. Do not allow the mixture to simmer.

The butter should have melted and the sugar fully dissolved. Increase the heat a little until it begins to simmer, then simmer for 5 seconds so that it reaches exactly 75 degrees and then remove from the heat. Pass the mixture through a sieve into a bowl.

Cover with cling film to avoid a skin forming, and then place in the fridge for 30 minutes.

Once cooled, pour into the centre of the tart case and then back in the fridge for at least 1 hour before serving. Serve with crème fraiche and raspberries.

Amaretto & Ginger Cheesecake

Base:

100g ginger nuts biscuits
40g butter, melted

Blitz the biscuits to a fine crumb and then mix with the melted butter until fully combined.
Add the crumb to the base of a tin and press down. Place in the fridge to set.

Cheesecake mixture:

200g cream cheese
150g mascarpone
100g icing sugar
3 gelatine leaves, soaked in cold water for 4 minutes
1 tbsp grated ginger
3 tbsp amaretto

Mix the cream cheese, mascarpone, icing sugar, and ginger together until fully combined.
Drain the gelatine leaves from the water and add to a small pan with the amaretto; gently heat until the gelatine has dissolved.
Stir the gelatine mixture through the cheesecake mixture.
Pour this onto the biscuit base and place back in the fridge.
Allow to set for a couple of hours.

To serve:

Zest of 1 lemon

Remove the cheesecake from the fridge and grate over the lemon zest.
Slice the cheesecake as required.

Chocolate & Orange Fondant

150g butter, bit more for greasing
135g 70% chocolate
90g flour, split into 25g and 75g
25g cocoa powder
3 eggs
3 egg yolks
200g sugar
1 tbsp orange juice
Zest from ½ orange
1 piece chocolate orange
4 tbsp crème fraiche

Makes 4:

Preheat the oven to 180 degrees.
Grease 4 dariole moulds with some butter.
Mix together the 25g of flour plus the cocoa powder and coat the inside of the moulds. Place them on a baking tray, ready for filling.
Over a Bain Marie, melt the butter and chocolate; stir occasionally.
Remove the melted butter and chocolate from the heat and sift in the flour, then whisk until combined.
In a separate bowl, whisk together the eggs, yolks, and sugar until fully combined.
Whisk the egg mixture into the chocolate mixture until smooth and fully combined.
Pour the chocolate evenly into the greased and dusted moulds.
Bake for 9 minutes. They are ready when you shake them, and only the middle moves a little.
Remove from the oven and then ease a knife around the edge to loosen.
Turn over each mould onto a serving plate and then serve each one immediately with 1 tablespoon of crème fraiche.
Grate over some chocolate orange.
Finish with a little orange zest.

Madeleines of Lemon & Thyme

65g butter
2 eggs
60g caster sugar
Pinch of salt
85g plain flour
1/2 tsp baking powder
Zest of ½ lemon
2 tsp thyme leaves
75g icing sugar
5 tsp lemon juice

Melt the butter in a saucepan until brown and then allow to cool.
Brush some of the butter into the madeleine tray and then dust with flour, tip out the excess, and place in the fridge to set.
Whisk together the sugar, salt, and eggs until frothy and starting to thicken.
Fold in the flour, baking powder, lemon zest, and thyme leaves.
Gradually drizzle in the remaining butter (save a little if making more than one batch).
Cover and place in the fridge for 1 hour.
Preheat the oven to 200 degrees.
Remove the batter from the fridge and fill each hole about 75% full, and don't smooth this over.
Bake for 10 minutes until golden brown, and then turn them out of the pan and place on a cooling rack to cool.
While cooling, pass the icing sugar through a sieve and mix with lemon juice to make a glaze.
Once cooled, brush the madeleines with the glaze and allow to set on the cooling rack.

Lime & Mint Panna Cotta

Panna cotta

150ml double cream
100ml milk
30g sugar
Drop vanilla essence
½ tsp agar agar
1 tsp lime juice
Lime zest
Mint leaves, finely chopped

In a dariole mould, add the lime zest and mint to the bottom.
Place all the other ingredients into a pan and heat up to 97 degrees whilst stirring.
Pass through a sieve and return to a clean pan, not on the heat.
Continue stirring until the mixture reaches 50 degrees.
Pour into the mould and place in the fridge.
Leave for a couple of hours to set.
When ready, remove from the fridge and turn over the mould onto a dessert plate, and the panna cotta should slide out with a gentle tap. If need be, tease it out with a knife.

To serve:

½ digestive biscuit, blitzed to a fine crumb
Slice of pineapple, cut into a fine dice
1 tbsp toasted coconut flakes
Lime zest
Mint leaves, finely chopped

Sprinkle some of the biscuit crumb alongside the panna cotta and add the pineapple and coconut flakes.
Finish with lime zest and mint leaves.

Lemon & Pistachio Financier

110g butter
25g pistachios, blitzed to a crumb
Zest of 1 lemon
43g plain flour
50g ground almonds
125g icing sugar
104g egg whites

Financiers

Grease the financier baking tray and chill in the fridge until needed.
Add the butter to a small pan and gently melt until it turns golden brown.
Mix together the pistachios, lemon zest, flour, ground almonds, and icing sugar.
Gently stir the egg whites into the flour mixture.
Next, add the butter and stir to form a batter.
Cover the bowl with cling film and place in the fridge for 1 hour.
Preheat the oven to 200 degrees.
Spoon the batter mix into the financier tray until about 7/8 full.
Bake for 10 minutes until firm to the touch and golden.
Leave to cool in the tray for a few minutes before removing to a wire rack.

100g icing sugar
2 tsp lemon juice

To finish

Pass the icing sugar through a sieve and then mix with the lemon juice to form the icing.
Place in a piping bag.
Once the financiers have fully cooled, drizzle over some of the lemon icing.

London Cheesecake

300g ready made puff pastry
50g smooth jam (F&M strawberry Champagne jam or similar)
55g butter
55g sugar
1 egg
40g ground almonds
1 tbsp flour

Cheesecake

Preheat the oven to 200 degrees.
Roll out the pastry and cut in half.
Place one piece of the pastry onto a baking tray lined with baking paper.
Spoon the jam evenly over the pastry on the baking tray.
Make a frangipane by creaming together the butter and sugar. Add the egg and stir to combine. Finally add the ground almonds and flour and stir through.
Add the frangipane mixture on top of the jam on the pastry and spread evenly.
Top the frangipane with the remaining pastry.
Bake the cheesecakes for 20 minutes.
Remove from the oven and allow to cool.
Slice into rectangular portions to serve.

200g icing sugar
4 tbsp water
Shredded coconut
150ml whipping cream

To serve:

Whip the cream until stiff and add to a piping bag with a narrow nozzle.
Make an icing with the icing sugar and water and add this to the top of a cheesecake.
Sprinkle over some shredded coconut.
Finish with some piped cream and serve.

Shortbread, Jam & Burnt Meringue

75g butter
38g icing sugar
75g flour
38g cornflour
Drop of vanilla
Pinch of salt
Sugar for sprinkling

Shortbread

Cream together the butter and icing sugar until fully combined.
Add the vanilla and salt, followed by the flours, and then mix until it all comes together.
Wrap the mixture in cling film and place in the fridge for 10 minutes.
Roll out the dough on a floured surface to about 1 cm thick; cut into neat rectangles about 4 cm x 6 cm.
Place the biscuits onto a baking tray lined with baking paper and place back in the fridge for 25 minutes.
Preheat the oven to 180 degrees and then bake the biscuits for 16 minutes.
Remove, allow to cool on a wire rack, and then sprinkle over some sugar.

100g rhubarb (or other seasonal red fruit)
50g sugar
2 tbsp water

Jam

Cut the rhubarb into 1 cm pieces and place in a pan with the sugar and water. Bring to a boil and the reduce to a simmer.
Place the lid on and simmer for 10 minutes.
Remove the lid and stir the jam and allow to cool.
Once cooled, store in an airtight container.

90g egg whites (about 3 eggs)
¼ tsp cream of tartar
115g granulated sugar
Pinch of salt
¼ tsp vanilla extract

Blowtorch

Swiss meringue

Set up a bain marie and then remove the bowl from the saucepan.
Mix together all of the ingredients in a heatproof bowl.
Place the bowl over the simmering water and whisk continuously until the mixture reaches 71 degrees. It should feel smooth between your fingers.
Remove the bowl from the heat and then whisk with a hand mixer on a medium-high speed until the mixture cools down and holds stiff peaks; this should take roughly 4 minutes. The mixture should be thick and marshmallow like in consistency.
Place the meringue into a piping bag with a fluted nozzle, ready to squeeze onto the shortbread.

To serve:

Spread some jam evenly over the shortbread and then pipe on some meringue.
Lightly torch the meringue.

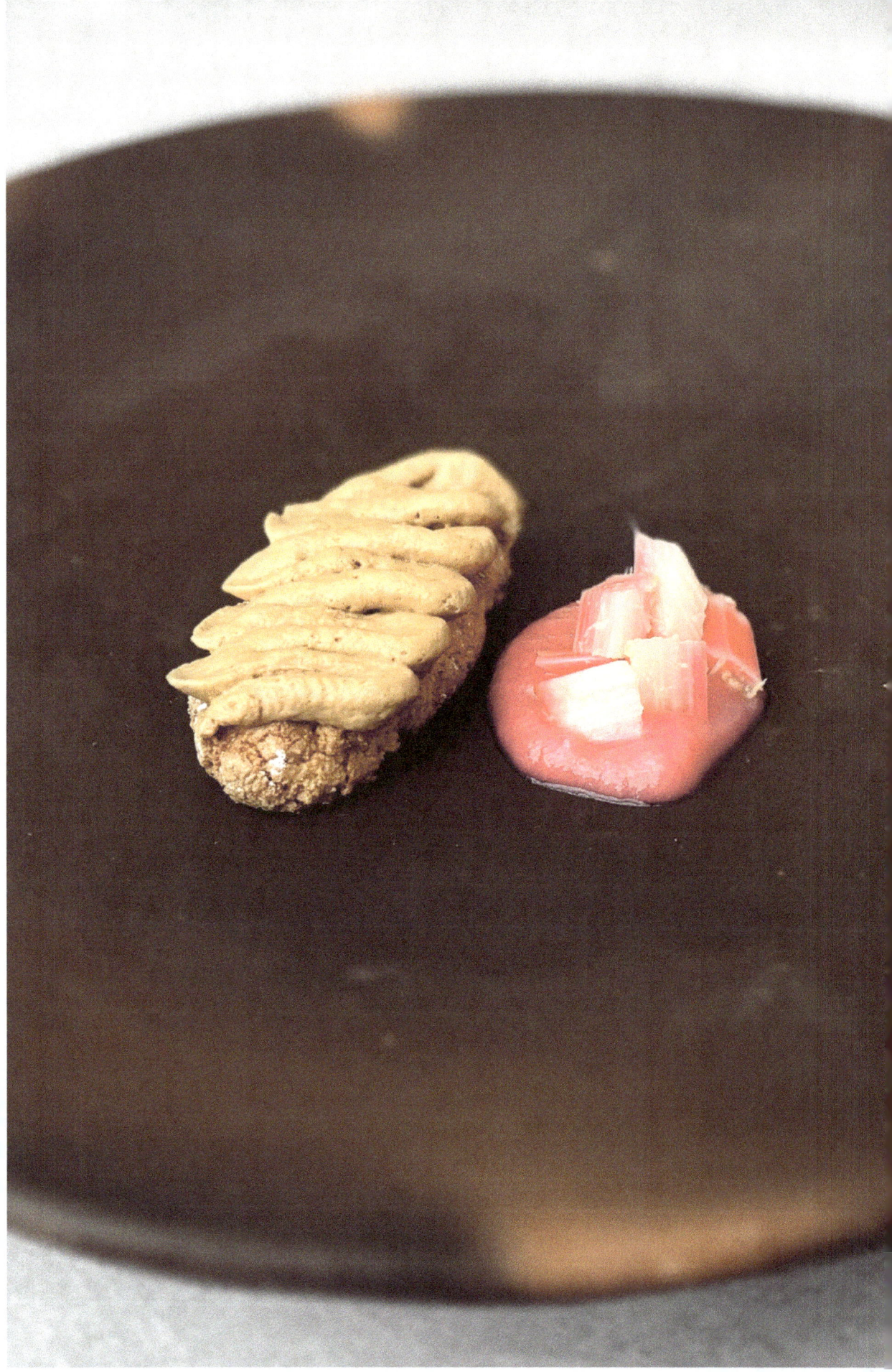

Amaretti & Basque Cheesecake

1 lemon
60g sugar
100g ground almonds
Egg white from 1 egg
1 tbsp amaretto liquor
30g icing sugar, plus some for dusting

Amaretti biscuits

Zest the lemon and rub half into the sugar until the mixture looks damp.
Set 1 tbsp to one side.
Add the ground almonds to the remaining sugar and stir to combine.
In a separate bowl, add the egg whites and whisk until stiff peaks form. Gradually whisk in the reserved tbsp of lemon sugar from above.
Mix half of the egg white and the amaretto liquor into the ground almond mixture until you have a smooth paste.
Fold in the remaining egg whites until just incorporated, and then chill for 1 hour.
Preheat the oven to 170 degrees.
Gently fold the remaining lemon zest, icing sugar, and lemon sugar into the chilled dough.
On a lined baking tray, spoon on the dough mixture into small rectangle shapes. Dust with a little icing sugar.
Bake for 14 minutes until slightly golden but still soft.
Remove and allow to cool on a wire rack.

Basque cheesecake puree

70g sugar
200g cream cheese
Pinch salt
1 egg
100ml double cream
10g flour
1 tbsp cornflour
2 sheets gelatine, dissolved in a little warm water

Preheat the oven to 220 degrees.
Cream together the cheese and sugar for 5 minutes.
Add the salt and then incorporate the egg. Whisk in the cream and then sift in the flour and cornflour and fold until fully combined.
Pour the mixture into a lined dish and cook for 40 minutes until well browned but still wobbly.
Allow to cool slightly, then blitz to a puree while still warm, adding the dissolved gelatine. Place into a piping bag.

Rhubarb

3 pieces of rhubarb, cut into 1 cm pieces
2 cm ginger, grated
Juice from 1 orange
1 tbsp sugar

Start with the poached rhubarb; in a small pan, add the ginger and orange juice and heat gently.
Pour the orange and ginger over 1/3 of the rhubarb and allow to infuse for 20 minutes. Remove and drain the rhubarb pieces.

For the sauce, place the remaining rhubarb into a small frying pan with the sugar and gently heat until syrupy. Allow this to cool, then blitz and pass through a sieve.

To finish

Pipe the cheesecake puree onto the amaretti biscuits.
Serve one on a plate and add some of the rhubarb sauce and poached rhubarb pieces alongside.

Tarte Bordaloue

Mini tart made with 1 pear, makes 3

Sweet pastry

175g flour
63g butter
62g sugar
1 egg, plus 1 yolk
Pinch of salt

Place the butter, sugar, and salt in a mixing bowl and mix with a wooden spatula.
Add the flour and the egg and mix until everything is bound together.
Place the dough onto a floured surface and work into a ball shape.
Wrap the dough in greaseproof paper and leave to rest in the fridge for at least 1 hour.
When ready, roll out the dough and line the tart case or cases as required, and blind bake at 180 degrees for 12 minutes. Remove and allow to cool.

Poached pears

Tin of pears

Cut each pear in half lengthways and then make incisions across the pear to allow it to fan out slightly.

Almond cream

125g butter
125g sugar
125g ground almonds
25g flour
1 ½ eggs
1 tbsp rum or poire liquer, or similar

Beat the butter until soft, and then add the sugar and ground almonds and continue mixing. Mix in some flour, then the eggs, and finally the rum.
Place in a small bowl and put in the fridge for 15 minutes.

To finish

Pear juices from tin
Icing sugar

Pre heat the oven to 180 degrees.
Half fill the pastry case or cases with almond cream and arrange a halved pear on top.
Bake for 25 minutes; the almond cream should be golden.
Remove and allow to cool in the tins for around 15 minutes, and then lift out of the tins.
Dust over a little icing sugar.
To finish, gently heat the pear juices and then lightly glaze over the top of the tart with a pastry brush.

Date Cake & Miso Caramel

Date cake

330g medjool dates
250g butter
95g muscovado sugar
1 egg

In a pan, melt together the dates and butter and then blitz until smooth.
In a bowl, whisk together the sugar and egg for a few minutes to create a sabayon.
Fold the date mixture into the sabayon.
Add the cake mixture into the cake tin or moulds and then cook at 150 degrees for 20 minutes; half way through, tap and turn the tray.
Allow to cool and then remove; before serving, they can be heated up in the oven for 4 minutes.

Vanilla ice cream

40g natural yoghurt
125ml full fat milk
45g double cream
60g sugar
50g egg yolks
Seeds from 2 vanilla pods
1 gelatine leaf

Soak the gelatine leaf in cold water.
Add the vanilla seeds to the double cream plus the milk, egg yolks, yoghurt, and sugar and heat in a saucepan until it reaches 82 degrees.
Add the soaked gelatine to the pan and stir until fully combined.
Chill the mixture over ice, stirring continuously to ensure an even spread of the vanilla seeds.
Place into a container and freeze.

Caramel sauce

7g haatcho miso
30g water
55g muscovado sugar
50g butter

Add all the ingredients except the butter to a pan and bring to a boil over medium heat while whisking to form a syrup. Remove from the heat, add the butter a little at a time, and whisk until fully combined.
Set aside in a small juicer.

To serve:

Add a piece of the warmed date cake to a bowl or plate.
Place a piece of ice cream on top and then spoon the caramel sauce over the top.

Fig & Orange Cheesecake

Base

120g digestive biscuits
50g melted butter
Pinch of salt

Bash the biscuits to a fine crumb and then mix with the melted butter and salt.
Press into the base of a cake tin and allow to set in the fridge.

Cheesecake

200g cream cheese
150g mascarpone
100g icing sugar
3 gelatine leaves
2 tsp lemon juice
Zest of 1 orange

Mix together the cream cheese, mascarpone and icing sugar.
Soak the gelatine leaves in cold water for around 5 minutes.
Add the soaked gelatine leaves to a small pan with the lemon juice and heat until fully dissolved. Stir this through the cream cheese mixture and add the orange zest.
Pour the mixture onto the biscuit base and place back in the fridge.

Orange jelly

125ml orange juice
1g agar agar
1 tbsp sugar

Heat all the ingredients in a pan until just boiling.
Remove from the heat and allow to cool enough to touch.
Pour over the cheesecake and place in the fridge to set fully.

Orange segments
Figs, quartered

Toppings

Once the jelly has set, portion the cheesecake into neat rectangles.
Top the cheesecake with alternate orange segments and quarters of fig.

Chocolate & Fig Oat Cookies

90g butter
50g sugar
50g brown sugar
1 eggs
1/2 tsp vanilla extract
120g flour
1/2 tsp bicarbonate of soda
1/2 tsp cinnamon
1/4 tsp salt
55g cup oats
75g dried figs
100g milk chocolate chunks

In a bowl, add the butter and sugars and beat until creamy.
Add the eggs and stir until combined, followed by the vanilla.
In another bowl, whisk the flour, bicarbonate of soda, cinnamon, and salt until combined.
A little at a time, add the dry mixture into the butter mixture and then stir in the oats.
Stir through the figs, followed by the chocolate chunks.
Place in the fridge for 90 minutes.
Pre heat the oven to 160 degrees.
Scoop out the dough into 1 tbsp rounds and place on a lined baking tray.
Bake for 12 minutes and then remove and allow to cool on a wire rack.

Pistachio Cake & Creme Chiboust

Pistachio cake

175g butter, softened
Pinch of salt
75g flour
140g pistachios, plus a bit extra to finish
1 tsp baking powder
100g sugar
2 eggs
2 tsp vanilla extract
2 tbsp milk

Preheat the oven to 160 degrees.
Grease a small cake tin and dust with a little flour.
Blitz the pistachios until just finely chopped.
Combine all of the ingredients until the mixture is creamy.
Fill the tin to about 2/3 full and bake for 20 minutes.
Leave to cool for 20 minutes, then remove and place on a wire rack.
Once cooled, slice the cake to the desired shape.

Crème Chiboust

2 gelatine leaves
125ml milk
½ vanilla pod
2 eggs, separated
50g caster sugar
13g cornflour

Soak the gelatine leaves in a small bowl of cold water.
Pour the milk into a pan and scrape in the vanilla seeds.
Bring the milk to a boil, then remove from the heat and leave to cool for 3 minutes.
In another bowl, whisk the egg yolks plus 25g of the caster sugar until pale; whisk in the cornflour.
Pour in the hot milk and slowly whisk until combined; pour back into the milk pan.

Bring the mixture back to the boil and whisk continuously over a medium heat for 2-3 minutes.

Squeeze the gelatine to remove any water, then add it to the pan and whisk until smooth. Remove from the heat and place in a bowl to cool to room temperature, covered in cling film.

Once the crème is cooled, tip the egg whites into a bowl and whisk to stiff peaks. Add the remaining sugar, half at a time, until the meringue is stiff and shiny.

Add a small amount of the meringue to the cooled crème and whisk thoroughly.

Fold in the remaining meringue and add to a piping bag with a fluted nozzle. Chill until needed.

To finish:

Add the piece of cake to a plate and sprinkle over some of the reserved pistachios.

Top with some piped crème and serve.

Pain Perdu & Chocolate

130g whole milk
130ml double cream
2 eggs
50g marmalade
½ tsp vanilla extract
Pinch of salt
200g croissants and/or brioche
45g melted butter

Pain perdu

Bring the milk and cream to a simmer. Blitz the marmalade, eggs, vanilla and salt. Slowly pour the warm milk over the egg mixture, whisking continuously and then allow to cool a little.
Preheat the oven to 160 degrees and line a small loaf tin with baking paper and grease lightly. Place the loaf tin in a Bain Marie, about halfway up the sides.
Crumble and break up the croissants/brioche and place in a bowl. In a pan, melt the butter then pour over the croissants/brioche and stir until fully coated. Next pour over the milk/egg mixture and stir well.
Tip the mixture into the loaf tin and press down. Cover in foil and tuck in the edges. Cook for 1 hour and it should be nearly set (wobbles a little, not too much); if not, cook for a little longer. Once ready, remove and allow to cool under a heavy weight, ideally overnight in the fridge but for as long as possible.
When ready, cut into squares that are roughly 6 x 2 cm; set to one side in groups of three and cut a little square out of the middle of one of the three pieces.
To assemble, see below,

Caramel filling

100g sugar
50g whipping cream
50g butter
Good pinch of salt

In a pan, melt the sugar until lightly golden. Add the cream in 3 stages, whisking after each addition.
Remove from the eat and add the butter a bit at a time and whisk until fully combined.
Finally add the salt and whisk through.
Place in a small bowl and allow to cool.

Chocolate orange coating

100g milk chocolate
1tsp orange juice

Melt the chocolate and orange juice over a Bain Marie to 45 degrees.
Pour ¾ of the chocolate onto a work surface and spread the chocolate around until it cools to 27 degrees.
Add the cooled chocolate to the remaining ¼ and mix thoroughly.
The mixture should be around 30 degrees; leave in a bowl.

Dark chocolate 'icing'

50g dark chocolate

Melt the chocolate over a bain marie and place in a piping bag.

Icing sugar

To assemble:

Take a set of three pieces of pain perdu. Place a whole piece on the work surface. Secondly, add the piece with the middle cut out.
Fill in the cut-out bit with the caramel filling.
Top with the third piece of pain perdu. Carefully dip this cube into the milk chocolate coating and allow to set.
Once set, drizzle over some of the dark chocolate icing.
Finish with a very light drizzle of icing sugar.

Serve as a snack, petit four, or as a small dessert alongside some whisky clotted cream.

Cinnamon Cracker & Cheddar

60g whole wheat flour
1 tsp ground cinnamon
Pinch of salt
20ml maple syrup
1 tbsp water
½ tsp coconut oil

Cracker

Preheat the oven to 180 degrees.
Whisk together the flour, cinnamon and salt.
Add the syrup, water and oil to the flour mixture and stir until a dough forms.
Roll out the mixture as thinly as possible and cut into circles, about 2½ cm.
Place on a silicone baking mat and prick each circle with a fork.
Bake for 14 minutes then remove and allow to cool.

Packet of cheddar cheese

Cheese

Cut the cheese into 2½ cm circles (and about 1 cm thick) to match the cinnamon crackers.
Core a hole in the middle of each cheese circle.

Apple gel

120ml apple juice
1 tsp thyme leaves, plus some extra for serving
1 tsp agar agar
Pinch of salt
Pinch of cinnamon
70g natural yoghurt

Add the thyme leaves to the apple juice and allow to infuse for around 30 minutes. Add the apple juice and thyme leaves to a saucepan and bring to the boil. Once boiling, add the agar agar, salt, and cinnamon and boil for 1 further minute. Pass the mixture through a sieve and pour into a shallow bowl and allow to set. Once set (about 10 minutes), blitz the apple gel with the yoghurt until smooth. Place into a piping bag and keep in the fridge.

To assemble and serve:

Place a piece of cheese onto a cracker.
Pipe some of the cool apple gel into the hole in the cheese.
Top with another cracker and serve on a small plate.
Finish with some reserved thyme leaves.

Meringue, Coffee & Autumn Fruits

Meringues

2 egg whites, at room temperature
Pinch of salt
110g caster sugar
¼ tsp vanilla essence

Preheat the oven to 120 degrees.
With an electric mixer, whisk the egg whites plus the salt until soft peak stage.
Slowly add the sugar, half a tablespoon at a time, whisking until the sugar has dissolved (the mixture shouldn't feel grainy to the touch). Continue until all the sugar has been added, then whisk for 2 minutes and add the vanilla essence.
Use 2 teaspoons to spoon the meringue onto a silicone mat into the desired shape.
Turn the oven down to 90 degrees and bake for 90 minutes.
Turn the oven off and leave the meriengues in the oven to cool completely. Remove and store in an airtight container until needed.

Hazelnut powder

50g hazelnuts, toasted
10g sugar
Pinch salt

Place all the ingredients into a food processor and blitz until smooth.

Coffee foam

1 mocha
1 tsp sugar

Add the sugar to the mocha and whisk well until foamy.
Serve immediately.

Chocolate sauce

90g milk chocolate

Melt the chocolate over a Bain Marie and use immediately.

To finish and serve:

Espresso powder
Dark chocolate, for grating
3 blackberries
3 raspberries
1 plum, cut into 6 pieces

Take 3 meringues and dust 1 in espresso powder, 1 in grated dark chocolate, and 1 in some hazelnut powder.
Start to plate by spooning some chocolate sauce onto a plate.
Next, sprinkle on some of the hazelnut powder.
Place the 3 dusted meringues onto the plate and then spoon on some of the mocha foam.
Finish by placing the fruit around the plate.

Crema Catalana

Crème brulee

284ml whole milk
½ orange, zest
½ lemon zest
1 cinnamon stick
1 vanilla pod
4 egg yolks
54g sugar
18g cornflour

In a pan, add the milk, orange zest, lemon zest, cinnamon stick, and vanilla.
Bring to the boil and leave to cool and infuse for 15 minutes.
In a separate bowl, whisk together the egg yolks and sugar, and then add the cornflour until pale and creamy.
Pass the milk through a sieve into a clean pan and add the egg yolk mixture. Bring to a medium heat and whisk continuously (around 4 minutes) until it thickens.
Pour into ramekins and allow to set in the fridge.

To finish

Orange zest
Lemon zest
Sugar

Remove the ramekins from the fridge. Sprinkle sugar over the top and then, with a blowtorch, heat the sugar until it melts and is golden; it should then harden.
Finish with some orange and lemon zest.

Pistachio Tiramisu

150g pistachios, shelled
190ml whole milk
30g butter
100g white chocolate
15g icing sugar

3 eggs, separated
100g sugar
250g mascarpone
2 tbsp coffee liqueur
150ml double cream
6 tbsp pistachio cream, from above
200ml strong black coffee
75ml Amaretto
300g sponge fingers
50g shelled pistachios, finely chopped
White chocolate for grating

Pistachio cream

Remove the ramekins from the fridge. Sprinkle sugar over the top, and then, with a blowtorch, heat the sugar until it melts and is golden; it should then harden.
Finish with some orange and lemon zest.

Tiramisu

Line a deep tin with parchment paper hanging over the sides to help lift it out.
Beat the egg yolks and sugar until pale and doubled in volume.
Add in the mascarpone and coffee liqueur and whisk for a further 2 minutes to fully combine.
In another bowl, whisk together the cream and 3tbsp of the pistachio cream until the mixture just holds its shape.

Fold the pistachio cream mixture into the mascarpone mixture.

In another bowl, whisk the egg whites to stiff peaks and then fold this into the mascarpone/cream mixture.

Place this into a piping bag and keep in the fridge.

In a shallow bowl, whisk together the coffee, amaretto and 2tbsp pistachio cream.

Dip the sponge fingers into this coffee mixture briefly, coating all sides and then arrange a single layer in the base of the tin.

Pipe over 1/3 of the cream mixture and grate on some white chocolate. Repeat this process twice more.

Chill in the fridge for minimum 4 hours or overnight.

To finish and serve, take 1tbsp of the pistachio cream and melt over a Bain Marie. Drizzle this over the top of the tiramisu and sprinkle over the pistachios. Remove from the tin, slice and serve.

Champagne Truffles

100ml whipping cream
110g dark chocolate (about 55% cocoa)
140g milk chocolate (about 40% cocoa)
30ml champagne
1.9g salt

50g cocoa powder
200g dark chocolate (about 70% cocoa)

- the truffles will keep in the fridge for 1 week in a sealed container or can be frozen for up to 1 month (defrost for a few hours).

Step 1:

Line a tray with baking paper.
In a saucepan, bring the cream to the boil.
Over a Bain Marie, melt together the chocolates.
Once the chocolates are melted, remove from the heat and whisk in a quarter of the hot cream. Gradually incorporate the rest, then add the champagne and the salt.
Pour the mixture into the lined tray and leave to set overnight in the fridge.
In the morning, turn out the set mixture and cut into 2 cm squares with a warm knife.

Step 2:

Pour the cocoa powder onto a small tray.
Melt the chocolate to 35 degrees.
Use two forks, one to lower the chocolate squares into the melted chocolate and one to turn in the cocoa powder.
Using a fork, dip each square into the warm chocolate, shake off any excess, and then coat in the cocoa powder, turning with the other fork.
Leave the squares in the powder on the tray until set hard.
Place the truffles into a sieve and shake off any excess powder.

Pineapple & Lime

1 pineapple

Pineapple

Top and tail the pineapple, then slice off the outer layer.
Cut the pineapple crossways into slices about 1 cm.
Cut out neat circles from the slices and reserve the offcuts, see below.
When ready, barbecue the pineapple until slightly charred on each side and softened.
While cooking, brush liberally with the syrup, see below.

Pineapple and lime syrup

Pineapple offcuts from above
Juice from 1/4 lime
2 tbsp sugar

Blitz the pineapple offcuts until smooth.
Place all the ingredients, including the pineapple, into a small saucepan and bring to a simmer.
Remove from the heat and allow to cool.

To finish and serve:

Pineapple and lime syrup from above
Lime zest
Coconut flakes, finely chopped
Coriander, leaves cut in half

Slice the barbecued pineapple into 4 pieces.
Brush some of the syrup onto a plate and place the sliced pineapple on top.
Grate some lime zest over the pineapple and finish with a sprinkle of coconut and coriander.

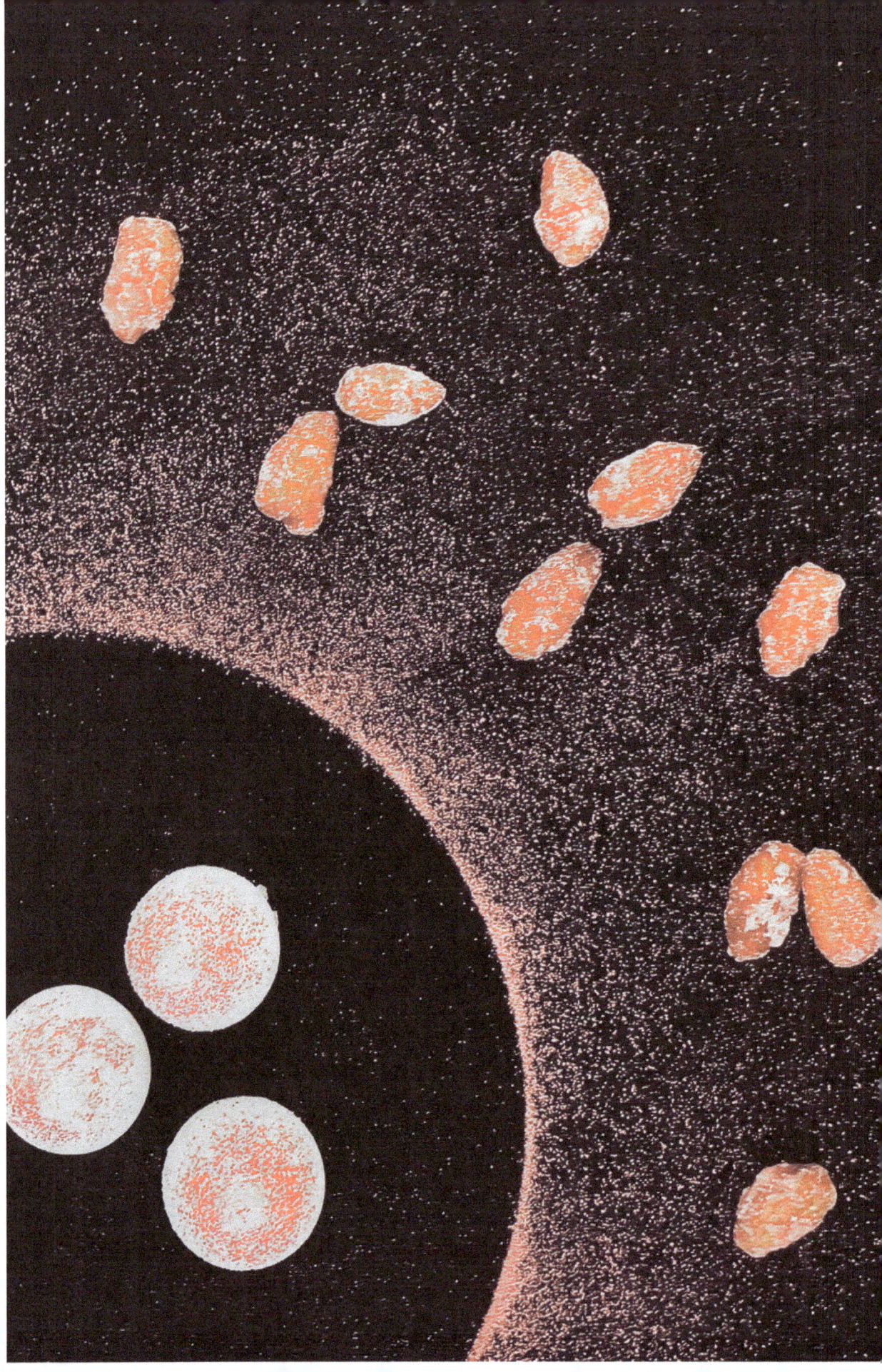

Pink Pralines

50g almonds
100g sugar
50ml water
Red food colouring, a few drops

Pink pralines

Preheat the oven to 190 degrees.
Bake the almonds for 10 minutes, then remove and turn the oven down to 70 degrees.
In a saucepan, heat the sugar and water; when boiling, add 3-4 drops of the red colouring.
Continue heating up to 124 degrees, then turn off the heat.
Add the roasted almonds and stir.
Pour out the mixture onto a silicone mat and collect the excess pink sugar.
Weigh the pink sugar and add more sugar as needed to get up to 100 g again.
Add the 100g of pink sugar plus another 50ml of water and repeat the steps above.
Repeat again for a third time, but this time at the end, instead of adding the almonds to the mixture, place the almonds into a metal bowl and pour the 124-degree mixture over them.
Shake well and then pour onto a silicone mat and bake for 30 minutes at 70 degrees.
Remove and allow to cool.

Edible pink dust
Small meringues
Brushed lightly with water

To finish and serve

Dust a plate with the pink dust.
Sprinkle some of the pink sugar over the meringues and add to a plate.
Add the pink pralines and sprinkle with a little pink sugar.

Choux au Craquelin

Craquelin

25g plain flour
25g sugar
20g butter

Mix the flour, sugar and butter together to form a dough.
Roll out the dough to 2mm between 2 pieces of parchment paper and place in the freezer for 30 minutes.
Once frozen, cut out 4cm rounds and return to the freezer.

Choux pastry

30g butter
Pinch of salt
½ tsp sugar
60ml water
20g flour
23g strong white bread flour
1 large egg

Preheat the oven to 180 degrees.
In a saucepan, add the butter, salt, sugar and water and cook over a medium heat.
When the butter has melted, add the flours and stir quickly with a wooden spoon until a dough forms.
Turn the heat down to low and stir vigorously for 2 minutes.
Transfer to a bowl and keep stirring until it stops steaming.
Add the egg and beat until fully absorbed.
Transfer to a piping bag and pipe balls roughly 5cm in diameter on a lined baking tray.
Top each ball with a piece of craquelin (from the freezer) and bake for 35 minutes until golden brown and crisp. Turn the oven off but leave the choux to dry out for another 30 minutes.

Remove and allow to cool.
Once cooled, slice off the top 1/3 ready to fill with the cream.

Chantilly cream

110g whipping cream
40g icing sugar
1/2 tsp vanilla extract
40g mascarpone

Place all the ingredients into a bowl and the whisk until the desired consistency is achieved (quite thick).
Transfer to a piping bag with a fluted nozzle.

To serve:

Milk chocolate shards
Strawberries, finely sliced
Mint leaves, finely sliced

Pipe some of the cream onto the bottom part of the choux bun.
Carefully place some milk chocolate shards, pieces of strawberry and mint leaves into the cream.
Top the cream with the top part of the choux bun.

Chocolate Marquise & Miso Cremeux

150g 70% dark chocolate
75g butter
75g sugar
3 tbsp cocoa powder
3 egg yolks
225ml double cream

Chocolate marquise

Melt the chocolate over a bain marie.
In another bowl, beat together the butter and half of the sugar until light and creamy.
Next, beat in the cocoa powder.
Beat together the other half of the sugar with the egg yolks until pale and creamy.
In another bowl, whisk the cream until thickened to a soft peak stage.
Pour the melted chocolate into the butter mixture and stir until thoroughly combined.
Fold in the egg mixture, followed by the whipped cream.
Line a narrow tin (small loaf tin) with three layers of cling film, leaving a 10 cm overhang.
Spoon the mixture into the tin and then fold over the excess cling film and place in the fridge overnight.
Before serving, place in the freezer for 10 minutes beforehand and slice with a warm, serrated knife.

100ml whole milk
100ml double cream
2 egg yolks
40g sugar
0.5g salt
145g good quality white chocolate
20g butter
15g haatcha miso

Miso cremeux

In a saucepan, heat the milk and cream until steaming.

In a bowl, whisk together the egg yolks, sugar, salt and miso until smooth and pale. Carefully pour in about half of the hot milk/cream and whisk continuously.

Pour the egg mixture into the pan of the remaining milk/cream and whisk well.

Over a low heat, cook the mixture while stirring with a spatula until thickened (maybe 4-5 minutes and 82-85 degrees).

Break up the white chocolate and place in a bowl.

Pour the hot custard mixture through a sieve over the chocolate. Cover the bowl and leave for 1 minute.

Uncover and stir the mixture until the chocolate has fully melted.

Add the butter and stir to fully mix in. Finally, blend with a stick blender to fully emulsify the mixture.

Cover with cling film to cool and then place into a piping bag and keep in the fridge; bring up to room temperature before serving.

Hazelnut crumb

25g roasted hazelnuts

Finely chop the hazelnuts.

To serve:

Place a slice of the marquise onto a plate. Pipe on some miso cremeux finish by sprinkling over some hazelnuts.

Lemon Parfait & Meringue

Lemon parfait

2 lemons, juiced
2 eggs
80g cater sugar
60ml double cream

Whisk the lemon juice, eggs, and sugar together in a large bowl until the sugar has dissolved, then whisk in the double cream to fully combine.
Preheat the oven to 160 degrees and line steel pastry rings with cling film.
Pour 65g of the parfait mixture into each ring and place into a roasting tin.
Half fill the roasting tin with hot water and cook for 45 minutes or until the parfait has set.
Remove and leave to cool.

Lemon shortbread

100g butter
50g icing sugar
100g plain flour
50g cornflour
1 tsp lemon zest
Pinch of salt

Preheat the oven to 160 degrees.
Cream together the butter and icing sugar.
Add the flour, salt, and lemon zest and bring the mixture together.
Form into a ball and leave in the fridge for 20 minutes.
Remove from the fridge and roll out to about 4 mm.
Cut into rounds the same size as the parfait pastry rings.
Place onto a lined baking tray and place in the fridge for 15 minutes.

Cook for 15 minutes and then remove and cool on a wire rack.
To finish, dust with a little icing sugar and lemon zest.

Meringue

100g sugar
120ml water
2 egg whites
Juice from ½ lemon

In a saucepan, mix the water and sugar and heat over high heat.
Once boiling, do not stir.
Heat up to 115 degrees.
Meanwhile, mix the egg whites and lemon juice in a bowl with an electric whisk to soft peaks.
Once the sugar mixture reaches 115 degrees, slowly drizzle it into the egg whites and keep whisking to soft peaks.
Transfer the meringue to a piping bag.

Limoncello sauce

75g sugar
30ml water
20ml limoncello
10g honey

In a pan, heat the water and sugar over a low heat until a golden caramel is achieved.
Remove from the heat and add in the limoncello and honey; stir to incorporate and be careful as it may spit.
Return the pan to the heat and bring to a boil then reduce to a simmer.
Reduce the sauce by about half then remove and allow to cool.
Transfer to a squeezy bottle.

Lemon verbena leaves, finely chopped

To serve:

Squeeze some of the limoncello sauce onto a plate into the desired shape or pattern. Place a circle of parfait onto a piece of shortbread and add to the plate. Squeeze over some meringue and finish with some lemon verbena.

CHOCOLATES ORANGES
£8.00/KG
SPAIN

Caviar | noun | ka·vi·ar |
    the pickled roe of sturgeon or other la[rge fish eaten]
    as a delicacy.

Confit | noun | kon·fi |
    meat (such as goose or duck) that ha[s been cooked]
    in its own fat and preserved

Flambe | noun | flom·bay |
    when a chef sets your food on fire [and they]
    meant to do it.

Scallop | noun | skol·lup |
    an edible bivalve mollusc with a [fan-shaped]
    shell. Scallops swim by rapidly o[pening and closing]
    the shell valves.

Truffle | noun | truhf·uhl |
    a strong-smelling underground [fungus that resembles]
    an irregular, rough-skinned po[tato, found chiefly]
    in broadleaved woodland.

Umami | noun | oo·mar·mi |
    a category of taste in food (be[sides sweet, sour, salty]
    and bitter), corresponding to [the flavour of glutamates,]
    especially monosodium glu[tamate].

Wagyu | noun | wa·gyu |
    meat from a japanese cow [which]
    is very tender, soft and eas[y to eat]

The Good Food Index

A
Albufera sauce 11
Amaretto 257, 264, 280
Anchovy 69, 80
Asparagus 209
Aubergine 92, 140

B
Beef 131, 182, 186, 233
Beetroot 4, 126
Black garlic 224
Brandy 52
Brie 92, 103
Brussels sprouts 156
Butternut squash 171, 178, 213

C
Cashew nuts 14
Cauliflower 139, 229
Cavolo Nero 125
Celeriac 6, 125, 155
Champagne 320
Champagne jam 274
Charcoal powder 68, 69, 162, 182
Cherries 49
Chestnut puree 154
Chicken skin 107
Chilli oil 79
Cod 107, 146
Crab 98, 134

D
Duck 212
Duck fat 130

F
Fava beans 64
Figs 293, 296
Foie Royale 110
Furikake 174

G
Gooseberry 194
Gorgonzola 170

H
Ham hock 72
Harissa 198, 199

I
Iberico ham 90

J
Jasmine rice 228
Jerusalem artichoke 124, 248
Juniper berries 125

L
Lamb 48, 138, 162, 198
Lemon verbena 338
Limoncello 337
Lobster stock 38

M
Macadamia nuts 57
Mackerel 74, 75
Madeira 10, 201
Mango 99
Medio dates 288
Miso 166, 202, 289, 333
Monkfish 122, 178, 224, 228
Mussels 36

N

Noilly prat 38, 60
Nori powder 148, 174, 220, 222

O

Octopus 64
Orange 266, 293, 314

P

Pear 256, 257, 284
Pearls 103
Pecan nuts 244, 245
Pheasant 122, 154
Pigeon 4, 124, 135
Pineapple 270, 322
Pistachio 92, 138, 146, 272, 298, 316
Pork 158, 224
Pork 78, 216, 236
Potato airbag 159
Prawns 32, 52, 60, 61
Prunes 158
Purple sprouting broccoli 209

R

Raspberry vinegar 234
Rhubarb 276, 281
Rum 285

S

Salmon 220
Salmon skin 28, 33
Scallop 6, 10
Sea bass 174
Sherry vinegar 53, 155
Shio Koji 202
Spelt flour 24, 106
Steak 166, 202

Strawberry 274, 329

T

Tamari 182
Truffle 18, 44, 56, 57, 82, 83, 155, 156, 234
Tuna 86, 194

V

Venison 4, 128, 131

W

Walnuts 256
Wasabi 194

The Cover Picture

Inman Ramen 2.0
Oil on Canvas
Rydal Hanbury

Rydal Hanbury is an artist from St Albans, known for her paintings including the city centre, the market stalls, and the characters in the city. Rydal appeared on Sky Arts 'Landscape Artist of the Year in 2024.

I met Rydal whilst she was sketching a pizza van in town on market day, and we have kept in touch since then.

Rydal has been a great supporter of my cooking projects, and when she commented, "Now that I could paint," about my ramen dish (see page 236), I was quick to take her up on her offer.

The painting beautifully captures the dish, and I am honoured to have Rydal's artwork associated with my book, and I am so grateful to her for painting it.

I can't think of a better front cover for this book.

Thanks Rydal!

www.ingramcontent.com/pod-product-compliance
Lightning Source LLC
Chambersburg PA
CBHW081613100526
44590CB00021B/3428